CONFLICT RESOLVED?

CONFLICT RESOLVED?

A CRITICAL ASSESSMENT OF CONFLICT
RESOLUTION

Alan C. Tidwell

PINTER
London and New York

Pinter
A Cassell Imprint
Wellington House, 125 Strand, London WC2R 0BB, England
370 Lexington Avenue, New York, NY 10017-6550, USA

First published in 1998
Reprinted 1999

British Library Cataloguing-in-Publication Data
A catalogue record for this book is available from the British Library.

ISBN 1-85567-542-0 (hardback)
     1-85567-543-9 (paperback)

Library of Congress Cataloging-in-Publication Data
Tidwell, Alan, 1958–
     Conflict resolved? : a critical assessment of conflict resolution
     Alan C. Tidwell.
          p. cm.
     Includes bibliographical references and index.
     ISBN 1-85567-542-0 (hardcover). — ISBN 1-85567-543-9 (pbk.)
     1. Conflict management.   2. Social conflict.   I. Title.
HM136.T53   1998
303/6'9–dc21   97–49099
                                                                            CIP

Typeset by BookEns Ltd, Royston, Herts.
Printed and bound in Great Britain by
Biddles Ltd, Guildford and King's Lynn

CONTENTS

Foreword *by Professor A. J. R. Groom*   vii

Acknowledgements   x

Preface   xi

1   The Challenge of Conflict Resolution   1

2   Popular Conceptions of Handling Conflict   19

3   Assumptions and Meanings in Conflict Resolution   30

4   Theories and Theorists in Conflict Resolution   60

5   Communication and Conflict Resolution   86

6   History and Conflict Resolution   107

7   Enemies   126

8   A Critique of Resolution Processes   147

9   Where to from Here?   171

Index   178

FOREWORD

Alan Tidwell has set out his stall to be provocative, but his excellent volume is so replete with good sense that it is hard to dispute many of his arguments. He claims, too, that he has not always given both sides of the argument. But that likewise is frequently not the case. It is true that his approach is a 'no-nonsense' one, which may disturb those who have a moral commitment to non-violence and peace above all else, or evangelical theorists, as Tidwell calls them, who value conflict resolution at all costs. I suspect, however, that most people will find this a balanced, well-informed, thought-provoking, clear and convincing analysis.

The resolution of conflict is a subject about which we all know something, since we experience it regularly in our daily lives. Often we do not notice that this is happening. Just as Monsieur Jourdain was unaware that he was speaking prose, so we are often unaware that we are engaged in conflict or conflict resolution. It is, after all, a sign of life to be in conflict. A person or society without conflict is dead. Conflict is the means by which we learn through feedback from the environment of other people. Whether or not we respond to that feedback determines whether the conflict will take a functional or dysfunctional turn. It is the business of the conflict resolutionists to explain why it is possible in theory, if not always in a particular time and place, to arrive at what John Burton, Alan Tidwell's mentor, calls a 'win–win' situation. For his part, Alan Tidwell is realistic: he knows that theory cannot always be readily translated into practice, but at least the notion of conflict resolution is something for which realistically we can aim.

In everyday parlance, the terms 'conflict settlement' and 'conflict resolution' are often used as synonyms, but in this monograph they reflect a clear difference in motivation and goal. For those who see human beings, both individually and in groups, as being driven to dominate each other or as living in an anarchical society in which their security dilemma can only be resolved through self-help, the best that can be hoped for is a settlement of conflict. In a *settlement* the strong impose a period of order and stability for the benefit of all, but chiefly themselves, and they are able to sustain it for as long as their coercive abilities last. For a conflict to be resolved it is necessary to go beyond that, and, indeed, a conflict settlement may be an impediment to a resolution, as in the case of Cyprus. In a *resolution* a new set of relationships are established between the parties, which are acceptable to them, in full knowledge of all aspects of the case, without any coercion of a manifest or structural character. It is the means of moving to the latter that is the theme of Tidwell's book.

Alan Tidwell clearly knows his onions. He has mastered the literature of conflict studies and has an impressive familiarity with a wide range of the social sciences, including psychological and anthropological approaches to conflict. In short, he is that new sort of scholar – one educated in conflict studies, which range from the study of the individual to the study of the global society through all the disciplines. He is native to the field in ways that the founding fathers could not be. This is, therefore, a young man's book, but that of a wise young man, which is not a contradiction in terms. In reading this book, I was reminded of that excellent series *Que sais-je?*, which makes such a valuable contribution to French intellectual life. It consists of authoritative studies, written for intelligent people who are not experts in a particular field by specialists in that field. They are no mere vulgarizations, yet cover much in a short compass. They require a real command of the subject, and it is Alan Tidwell's achievement to have emulated them.

One way or another we are brought face to face with a host of difficult but important questions. We can hardly read this book without thinking about our own views of the nature of human relations and the implications therefrom. We might ask ourselves why some conflicts get dressed up in another form; for example, the ethnicization of what may be an economic conflict. We must ask ourselves whether you can win by using coercive means, in the short run or in the long run – a question which is highly relevant when dealing with Saddam Hussein. We may wonder why the seemingly weak may sometimes prevail. Moreover, should we try to empower the weak or disempower everybody so that we can get to the heart of the problem by making the issue the central element of analysis rather than the relative power configurations of the parties to the conflict? Conflict resolution, in an academic sense, is very much a

Western subject, but what is the role of culture in conflict, and how do other cultures manage their conflicts? Is the notion of some conflict researchers, such as John Burton, that everyone has basic human needs which are not in short supply merely a comfortable rationale for conflict resolution or a basic, hard-nosed reality? Can we differentiate such basic human needs from things that we merely want rather than actually need? If so, what is the mediating effect of culture on such needs? What is the role of rationality in conflict, and the importance of language and communication? Above all, how do we use history, and how can we escape from it? For, if we are to resolve a conflict with bitter history, particularly a protracted conflict, then we must in some sense, while not denying history, decouple ourselves from it. To do otherwise will allow the past to determine the future, which is not the name of the game. Finally, how do we look at adversaries? Are their problems more important than ours because they are only a problem to us while they cannot resolve their own difficulties?

These are but a few of the range of problems that spring to mind when reading Alan Tidwell's book. We must find our own answers, but his cogent analysis of the literature and clear presentation of his own ideas put us in Tidwell's debt, even if they do not remove the question mark from *Conflict Resolved?*

A. J. R. Groom
University of Kent at Canterbury

ACKNOWLEDGEMENTS

I would like to thank David Ardagh and Suzanne Murray for urging me to publish this manuscript. I am also most appreciative of the efforts of my editor, Petra Recter, who persisted in getting the final product out. Intellectually, this manuscript owes much to Frank Astill, John Burton, John Groom, Andrew Heys, John Hunt, Abdul Latif Kamaluddin, George Kurien, Dennis Sandole and Greg Tillett.

My particular thanks are for my family: parents, wife and children. Thanks for all your support.

PREFACE

This text is written as a provocation. I have not included every side to an argument; readers should supply their own refutations of my claims. Nor have I provided readers with an exhaustive list of every model or theory of conflict resolution – that would not necessarily be a fruitful exercise. Rather, my task is to provoke readers into critically assessing their own beliefs, assumptions and values pertaining to conflict and its resolution. Perhaps my primary motivation to write this text was to respond to two classes of written material in the field, the positive peacemaking and the evangelical theories.

Positive peacemaking is a process informed by the moral commitment to non-violence and peace. Positive peacemaking is a good thing, but it can be carried too far. Not all conflicts can or should be resolved; frankly, there are some conflicts I do not wish to resolve – I want to win them. For me, these conflicts are about justice, about right and wrong, to name a few. Any honest reflection will unearth these sorts in readers' lives too. I believe that those who write too glibly or positively about conflict resolution simply do not take into account some very real and very deeply seated issues.

A second source of motivation comes from the evangelical theorists. These are writers who propagate the value of conflict resolution at all costs. They appear so motivated to sell their theory that they remove it from reality. I believe that some theorists go too far in proclaiming an answer to the problem of conflict. I do not claim to have written anything like the definitive text in the field; it has its own problems, but I do believe that you will find here guidance as to where some flaws in the field lie. Finally, an assumption made in writing this text is that the audience has some basic knowledge about conflict resolution. Most readers will probably have some acquaintance with the role of a mediator, a facilitator, and may know the essential steps to generic problem-solving. While readers may have this in mind, I will nonetheless outline my interpretation of the generic conflict resolution process, and identify the areas where social and structural issues are most prevalent. Those issues having been identified, the remainder of the text will examine each of those in turn.

1
THE CHALLENGE OF CONFLICT RESOLUTION

Human beings engage in conflict. Aggression, warfare, violence seemingly equate with the human condition. Equally, humans have sought, as long as there has been conflict, to handle conflict effectively, by containing or reducing its negative consequences. Treaties, cease-fires, agreements and handshakes are all symbols of human endeavours to reduce the negative consequences of conflict. Some attempts at reducing those negative consequences work better than others. Why? Why is it that in one instance a handshake and an apology may end weeks of enmity, whereas in another instance a handshake or apologies do absolutely nothing? The study of conflict resolution seeks to come to grips with explaining why people engage in conflict, and identify ways in which conflict may be resolved.

Conflict resolution is now recognized as a legitimate, indeed important, topic of academic study. Justification for the study of conflict resolution appears daily: rising levels of domestic violence in the post-war era, the birth and growth of nuclear stockpiles, and the increasing level of dissatisfaction with the status quo − these and a myriad of other concerns serve to galvanize attention on resolving conflict. Even before these modern-day ills, however, humanity has been locked into patterned ways of dealing with conflict. As Galbraith (1996, p. 3) comments, 'The real world has constraints imposed by human nature, by history and by deeply ingrained patterns of thought.' Conflict resolution, for some, appears to offer alternatives to what seems an otherwise dangerous and threatening world. Much of its focus has been on techniques or methods by which conflict may be handled. The focus has been largely upon individual actors, or a small collection of actors, working to resolve interpersonal, organizational or community conflict. International conflict resolution has also been an area of keen focus, but has been left largely to the diplomats and practitioners at the UN. The literature on conflict resolution focuses on 'how to do it', with scant attention paid to situational and contextual issues. Yet a more textured and mature approach to conflict resolution demands examination of these contexts and situations. Without an examination of those factors that constrain resolution, there can be no effective, long-term effort to resolve the more difficult social conflicts that face us today.

This text serves two purposes. First, it introduces the reader to the essential ideas found in the study of conflict resolution, but perhaps more important, it puts conflict resolution in context. The second purpose is important because the study of conflict resolution is largely inadequate, if and when it ignores the societal and structural constraints imposed on a given conflict situation. Conflict does not occur within a vacuum. Conflict resolution texts emphasize the imaginative, creative generation of alternatives, empowerment of the weak, and the search for non-violent change. Yet the search for alternatives, empowerment and non-violence occurs within a social and structural context. Problem-solving and conflict resolution cannot be removed from the social environment. For example, when scholars recommend that those seeking resolution of conflict focus on the problem and not the person with whom one is in conflict, they are making some very real and unhealthy assumptions about the nature of conflict. A peasant woman whose family has been killed by members of a rival ethnic group is unlikely to be able, or want, to separate the person and the problem. For her, the people are the problem. Often this is the reality in which many would-be conflict resolvers find themselves. One may wish to have her see that, in fact, her problem is not with the people she so bitterly despises, but with unsatisfied needs, hidden motivations and so on. It is, however, difficult and even questionable to engage in such a transfer of meaning. The question arises, what kind of thing will replace her hate of her enemies? What psychological, social or other concept will she be persuaded to adopt? In shifting her conceptual vision of where or whether her enemy resides, the third party may accidentally create a new and more powerful enemy. Then again, such a shift in meaning may be the only plausible way in which third parties can unlock a conflict. It is a risk that any third party must face, if resolution is a serious objective.

So, the task here is to present a picture of conflict resolution, within the context of many of the societal and structural constraints. The end result is that conflict resolution is a more difficult and challenging task than may sometimes be suggested.

A Simplified View of Conflict Resolution

Conflict resolution is best thought of in cyclical terms. Consider Figure 1.1. For convenience I will start with the question of functionality. Most people or institutions that consider using conflict resolution do so only after having asked the question, 'Is this a good conflict?' One can substitute the word 'good' with functional, valuable, profitable, useful, justifiable, and so on. The point remains that the decision to 'resolve' a conflict is a value choice, and is subjective. Even corporations appearing to be motivated by the 'bottom line' will make value choices about how long they will incur a loss before they will intervene; some companies will suffer financial loss for a long period if a given conflict meets other desired outcomes. This situation refers to the question of functionality: that is, when faced with a conflict and the possibility of resolution, parties will ask, 'Is it functional?' The answer, even when dressed with seemingly objective rationalizations, is ultimately subjective and value laden.

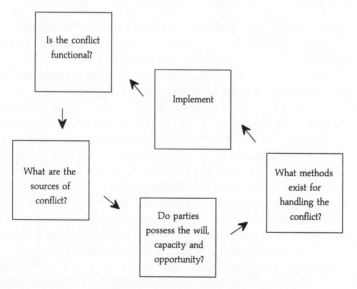

Figure 1.1 Conflict resolution seen as a cyclical process

After having decided, for whatever reason, that the conflict is 'non-functional', parties and interveners ask, 'What are the sources that drive this conflict?' This question is usually not asked in any existential manner; rather it is a very practical and goal-driven question. It may be restated as 'What are the sources of this conflict that I need to know about so that I can resolve it?' Given any conflict or problem there is a range of possible information about that conflict, a range that stretches from very little information to a vast array. The range of knowledge needed to engage in problem-solving is described by Simon as being within a 'bounded rationality', where one seeks information about a problem only to the degree that it will solve that problem (Simon, 1957). Clearly, though, the sources of conflict stretch far deeper than what any bounded rationality would consider. Much has been written about the origins of conflict, some arguing that conflict is in human nature and inherent to being human. Others argue that humans encounter conflict contingent upon social learning or social influence. There are, however, some very difficult questions that arise out of the search for causes, including the following:

- Can conflict be reduced to one or two causes?
- How does an intervener or party to the conflict know a cause?
- Does knowing a cause necessarily make resolution any easier?

Although identifying causes of conflict is loaded with problems, in practical terms interveners or parties are able either to identify the causes or to rationalize causation and move forward.

Parties or interveners must ask whether the necessary and sufficient conditions exist, or to what degree they exist, to facilitate resolution. Very simply, those conditions are opportunity, capacity and volition. For conflict to be resolved there must be the *opportunity* to do so; for example, there must be time to try to resolve conflict. A workplace where the employer will not allow parties time to discuss their conflicts is one where the opportunity for resolution is slim or non-existent. The origins of curtailed opportunity are found in many different places, ranging from intra- and interpersonal sources to societal and social limits on opportunity. A bad relationship with a boss reflects an interpersonal constraint on opportunity, whereas South African apartheid represented a societal source.

A second condition needed to resolve conflict concerns the *capacity* to resolve. Those in conflict must have the ability to resolve; that is, they must possess the skills and resources required for resolution. This is why communication is so often raised as being central to the resolution of conflict. Often, though, people confuse communication and resolution. Communication does not necessarily lead to resolution, because if parties communicate conflictual behaviour, then it appears that communication is fuelling conflict, not resolving it.

A final requirement for resolution is *volition*, or will. Without some desire to engage in resolution conflicts will persist. Desire may be from a humanitarian perspective, fatigue, or other sources. The will to resolve, or volition, certainly need not be benevolent. Parties do not have to like one another, they do not have to have goodwill or warm hearts; they may simply be tired of fighting. Whatever the motivation, parties must possess the volition to resolution.

If the conditions of volition, opportunity and capacity are non-existent, several possible outcomes emerge. One possible alternative is that conflict resolution may still be attempted, though obviously without success. A second alternative is that those trying to resolve the conflict will simply quit, making note of some of the difficulties to resolution. A third possible alternative is that some remedial action will be taken to alter the situation. In a workplace, the employer may be persuaded to create opportunities for employees to take the time to try to resolve a conflict. The persuasion, of course, may be through the good offices of an intervener, or through a strike or some other action. Parties lacking communication skills will receive training, or those lacking resources will be empowered through alliance with the more powerful or through inhibiting the power of the other party to the conflict. Finally, those lacking the volition may be persuaded through various means, ranging from moral suasion to the use of violence.

There are obvious problems encountered when conflict is considered in a larger sense. For example, how does one increase the conflict resolution skills of an entire society? How does one increase the resources of a weak party when the stronger party can veto such action? Finally, if a party is so filled with hate and loathing that an entire culture is predicated upon the vilification or enmification of one party, how can the volition for conflict resolution be created?

Equally, the question arises as to what extent these necessary and sufficient conditions need to be answered before one can move on. In group conflict, does the entire group need opportunity, capacity and volition, or does only the leadership need them? How much capacity is enough? Do they only need enough capacity to be able to engage in negotiation, even though they are likely to suffer badly? Or do they need a greater capacity? How does one know how much capacity a party has? The USA appeared to have ample capacity in fighting the Vietnam War, yet history proves otherwise. There are no meaningful objective measures of capacity, so that decisions about capacity are tenuous at best. The same difficulty exists around the issue of opportunity, in that the measures of opportunity are arguable. Yet the lack of objective measures should not dissuade the researcher, or the practitioner, from examining these factors.

Having examined the opportunities, capacities and volition of each party, one moves to identifying the methods for resolving conflict. These methods, generally, are well known and catalogued. They include negotiation, mediation and facilitation. Yet each method will be crafted to the specific situation – if not intentionally, then at least through the implicit assumptions of those intervening. This process of melding the ideas of practitioners and parties with real-life action is vital, and central to the process of conflict resolution. The manner in which theories about human behaviour in general and conflict resolution specifically are tied to behaviours is a central question in conflict resolution. The link between theory and action, or praxis, is profoundly influenced by societal and structural factors. Beliefs, values and culture all impact not only upon what one thinks, but upon the action taken. Therefore, while many methods of resolving conflict exist, they are limited by the world within which they operate.

The many texts on conflict resolution, acting as guides for how to resolve, present their case within a given context. More often than not it appears as if processes for handling conflicts are superimposed upon the context. For example, rather than examining the needs of the context, mediation is applied to a whole range of conflicts without due consideration of its appropriateness.

A further limitation on context is found in culture. Methods such as mediation or facilitation may not be appropriate within a given cultural context. This simple point is not, however, well discussed within the writings of conflict resolution. Yet it would seem obvious, for example, that in cultures in which to speak directly about a conflict is regarded as inappropriate, many Western methods would simply not work.

As Figure 1.1 shows, the final step in conflict resolution is to return from implementing a method for resolution to evaluating whether conflict is functional or non-functional. Once again, this is perhaps the most value-laden element of the process and one that requires the most reflection. One person's dysfunctional conflict is another's functional process. It depends largely upon the perspective, values and beliefs of those in conflict. Equally, the functionality of the resolution process is largely dependent upon the values, beliefs and perspectives of those involved.

In the final analysis, then, what is presented here is a very textured view of conflict resolution. Rather than advocating the methods of conflict resolution, as so many texts do, this is more a discussion of the factors that impact upon the resolution of conflict. Fundamental to this argument is the observation that resolving conflict is not a simple thing. If it were simple, then perhaps it would occur more often. Rather one examines the class, ethnic, gender and nationalist conflicts that have lasted for generations, and one may feel a strong sense of despondency about their eventual resolution. Yet positive steps towards resolution do occur, but against the backdrop of some of the things that have been mentioned here. The necessary and sufficient conditions to conflict resolution, for example, must be satisfied to some degree before progress can be made. Equally, accounting for the profound historical animosity that exists between peoples will go a long way towards providing practitioners of conflict resolution with a better understanding of the difficulties that lie before them.

One of the real difficulties in studying conflict resolution and its constraints lies within society and its structure. How does one gain access to a conflict? Most students of conflict resolution gain temporary access through clinical placements, short participant observation sessions, or action research projects. While this is a laudable step in the right direction, it is really quite insufficient for truly coming to grips with the profound nature of conflict. A major difficulty in studying conflict is that the researcher usually goes home. The student of conflict resolution rarely suffers the threat of the conflict in any long-term and enduring sense. Students may suffer a threatening or violent incident, but then they go home and are, hopefully, debriefed. Yet parties to conflict do not get such luxuries. This presents those who conduct conflict resolution research with some very real problems. Gaining a glimmering of an understanding may be better than none at all, but then again, a glimmering of an understanding may be just enough to give rise to some truly profound mistakes, as opposed to some obvious and stupid ones. As the saying goes, one may have just enough knowledge to be dangerous. These methods seem to be the best answers right now to the problem of understanding, though perhaps better ones have yet to be created. Possible ways of helping students understand conflicts include providing a good background briefing of where the potential hazards might lie.

In the remainder of this chapter a brief history of the development of Western conflict resolution is presented. This history provides the reader with a better understanding of the emergence of the field, where it began and perhaps where it is headed. In Chapter 2 the popular conception of conflict handling is considered. Chapters 3 and 4 focus on theory, with Chapter 3 examining the theoretical schools which spotlight the origins of conflict. Chapter 4 provides the reader with a brief overview of some of the major theorists of conflict resolution. Chapter 5 focuses on the role that communication and language play in both assisting and inhibiting conflict resolution. Chapter 6 examines the role of history, both as a source of motivation and as an analytical tool. Chapter 7 focuses on the process of enmity. Chapter 8 considers conflict resolution processes, specifically examining the ways in which values impact upon process. Finally, Chapter 9 provides the reader with some concluding thoughts on the nature of conflict resolution.

History of Conflict Resolution

The study of conflict resolution has been profoundly influenced by a variety of factors, ranging from the founding of the UN to the authorship of such popular books as *Getting to Yes*. Conflict resolution has its tradition in three different areas: organizational development and management science; international relations and the peace movement; and alternative dispute resolution. Each of these three traditions influenced and directed the course of modern-day conflict resolution. There have been, of course, many other sources of influence in conflict resolution, but these three represent the most consistent and powerful influences. Equally, there are many antecedents to the influences that are described below. One should not accept this brief history as being anything like complete; rather it is presented to provide the reader with a sense of where conflict resolution came from and where it is going.

The phrase conflict resolution means different things to different people, reflecting its varied historical development. Some see conflict resolution as any process by which conflicts are handled. This would include warfare, violence, management solutions, deterrence, contracts and so on. Others, however, have developed more narrowly defined meanings. Burton, for example, argues that conflicts concern

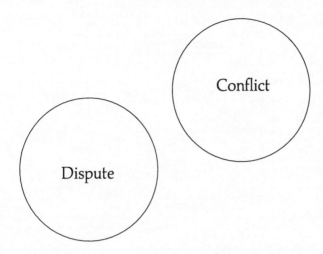

Figure 1.2 Burton's view of conflicts and disputes as separate processes

only situations where human needs satisfaction is denied. Resolution of such conflicts occurs only after relationships have been re-examined and realigned.

Burton's use of the term is narrowed further when he defines disputes as concerning negotiable interests. The process of conflict resolution, one concerning non-negotiable needs, differs markedly from dispute resolution, concerning negotiable interests. The test to differentiate conflicts and disputes is in action. This intellectual debate, over the scope of conflict resolution, reflects the difficulty in knowing whose history of conflict resolution is being examined.

Conceptually, Burton views conflicts and disputes as quite separate (see Figure 1.2). However, a logical problem exists, in that one cannot know whether a negotiation failed because of intransigence or bad negotiation behaviour, or whether it was due to the existence of non-negotiable needs.

It may be preferable to view the distinction between disputes and conflicts as a continuum (Figure 1.3), in which there exists no fine distinction between disputes and conflicts, rather only a difference of degree. Disputes are generally less intense over time and have a greater degree of negotiability, whereas conflicts are more intense over time and have a lesser degree of negotiability. Unsatisfied needs are found in conflicts, whereas disputes do not possess the same level of dissatisfaction.

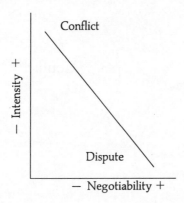

Figure 1.3 The dispute–conflict continuum

Keeping this brief discussion in mind, let us now turn to the emergence of the modern study of conflict resolution.

Organizational Development and Management Science

Anyone interested in making organizations work better, more smoothly or more efficiently has had to cope with the question of conflict. In the earliest days of management theory conflict was seen simply as inefficiency. Management theorists were interested in removing inefficiency created by the division between the employers and the employees. Conflict had its base in class divisions. Theorists sought ways of unifying the interests of the two groups. Frederick Taylor, for example, advocated in the early twentieth century a system known as Scientific Management, where through the use of scientific principles and time-and-motion studies workers could be given the one best way to do their job. The advocates of scientific management argued, 'It [the Scientific Management movement] will give people better understanding and co-operation, and realize a new policy, the policy of a human world' (Taylor, quoted in Mouzelis, 1981, p. 84).

Since then, however, the study of organizations has come a long way. Mary Parker Follett was a pioneer of the view that conflict had a positive place in organizations. Instead of trying to eradicate conflict from the workplace, she advocated using conflict positively.

She pleaded in 1925, 'As conflict – difference – is here in the world, as we cannot avoid it, we should, I think, use it. Instead of condemning it, we should set it to work for us. Why not?' (Follett, 1995). She believed that conflicts emerged from limited thinking, in which the only way to manage conflict was through compromise. Thus, in compromise, no party got what they wanted, rather only a portion of what they originally sought. She believed, on the other hand, that conflict could be constructively managed if parties thought outside expected or usual barriers. Constructively managed conflict was that which emanated from the invention of alternatives. She coined the term integration to refer to those solutions to conflict that invented solutions outside of expectation.

After Follett, however, there has been an explosion of writers who address the subject of conflict within an organization. Perhaps most notable are Robert Blake and Jane Mouton, authors of *The Managerial Grid*, first published in 1964. Scimecca (1991, p. 22) explains:

> They pointed to five ways of dealing with conflict. The first is withdrawal. A second way is to try and smooth over the differences that are seen as the basis of the dispute. Third, one or more parties to a conflict may force a win-or-lose resolution. The fourth way is the most commonly used approach, that of compromise. These four ways, however, are problematic, in that, with the possible exception of total withdrawal, the conflict will usually reoccur. In order to resolve conflicts so that they will not reoccur ... [the authors] advocated a fifth way, the use of a problem-solving attitude.

Since the publication of *The Managerial Grid*, problem-solving has become common language in management theory. Further developments in organizational conflict result in a view of conflict as a useful and increasingly important tool in the maintenance of a healthy organizational life. Robert Tanner Pascale, author of *Managing on the Edge*, has argued that conflict can often be a positive force in organizations. He writes:

> Problems [read conflicts], then, are not just hassles to be dealt with and set aside. Lurking inside each problem is a workshop on the nature of organizations and a vehicle for personal growth. This entails a shift: we need to value the process of finding the solution – juggling the inconsistencies that meaningful solutions entail. (Pascale, 1990, p. 263)

An organizational perspective on conflict is useful in any

discussion of societal and structural sources of conflict, inasmuch as writers in management science are developing important and useful conceptual tools for analysing conflict. Many of the processes of addressing conflict, such as mediation, arbitration and facilitation, grew in relation to their application to organizational needs. Mediation, for example, did not become commonly used in the USA until after the federal government brought mediation to the settlement of labour–management disputes. In fact, labour–management relations have played a major role in the evolution of methods for addressing conflict. Yet the usual discourse of labour–management relations has included little that aims at understanding conflict, but has focused on making conflict less costly and more efficient. The field of labour–management has done much to advance conflict resolution, inasmuch as it has acted as a very active and imaginative testing laboratory for new ideas on how to resolve conflict. The strength of organizational development has been in applying conflict resolution strategies to real-life situations.

International Relations and the Peace Movement

In the study of societal and structural sources of conflict the study of international relations has played a vital role. The UN Charter provides for the use of mediation and conciliation in the resolution of disputes. There can be no doubt that the United Nations, like its forerunner the League of Nations, has sought (with limited success) to create alternative methods for resolving disputes. Yet the UN has had only limited impact on conflict resolution. It has offered some glimmer of alternatives to the traditional models of handling conflicts, but it has failed to provide any truly systematic method for their resolution. Also, the track record of the UN in resolving conflicts has been so dismal that it is arguable that the organization has provided a model showing the alternatives to be avoided. A major criticism of it is that it has not really provided an alternative to power politics at all, but rather has provided only another method through which power politics may be played out.

Power was one of the key points of criticism offered by a group of international theorists. Burton (1986, p. 176) writes of this period:

> The academic community was sharply divided between those who adopted a traditional or power view, and those who adopted what was then termed the 'behavioral' view (not to be confused with the 'behavioral' or quantitative school of the 1960's). The latter sought to

determine, not how to settle conflict by the application of legal norms, but the nature of conflict and how to resolve it by an understanding of it by the parties concerned.

From the division within the academic community emerged a group of researchers who sought to 'falsify the proposition that disputing parties were unwilling to cooperate in resolving conflicts' (ibid., p. 176). One group of academics, under the aegis of the Centre for the Analysis of Conflict (CAC) and located at University College London, sought to investigate the sources of conflict. Examining conflict in Southeast Asia, CAC, with the cooperation of British prime minister Harold Wilson, brought together representatives of the governments of Malaysia, Singapore and Indonesia. CAC, without any governmental input, then began to run a 'controlled communication' meeting, in which parties were asked to explain the conflict. Burton and the other members of CAC created an environment not aimed at negotiation, but one characterized by explanation and analysis. These controlled communication workshops are also known as problem-solving workshops, facilitated workshops or simply workshops. The workshop relies upon a thorough understanding of small-group dynamics and the separation of the process of communication from the content of the material being discussed. As Burton (ibid., p. 177) comments of this early workshop experience, 'Whether connected or not it is impossible to say: but fighting stopped shortly afterwards.' Out of this work grew Burton's emphasis on human needs as the unit of analysis, replacing that of power.

Herb Kelman of Harvard University, who was involved with a CAC workshop on Cyprus, began to examine the role of problem-solving workshops in other conflicts, and apart from work done by CAC. The primary focus of Kelman's work has been the Middle East. Running roughly parallel in time to Burton's work was that of Leonard Doob of Yale University. Working independently, Doob also undertook to use workshops in the resolution process. His first foray into the use of workshops occurred in 1966, and focused on the resolution of border disputes.

Hill (1982, p. 111) explains that these workshops served two functions:

> (1) to provide conflict researchers with an opportunity to investigate the dynamics of an ongoing international conflict; and (2) to provide a setting in which the parties to the conflict could meet and learn

techniques that would enable them to resolve eventually the conflict peacefully.

While they have yet to become commonplace, the workshops have served a vital purpose. They break down traditional approaches to the resolution of conflict and offer alternative ways which operate outside the traditional power framework. A key component of the workshops is that of analysis. Unlike mediation, arbitration or other more traditional alternatives, the workshops promote analysis as a necessary precursor to resolution.

While the workshop movement was under way in the 1960s there was also a growing body of religious and peace activism. Although this area did not provide very much in the way of new conceptual insights into the resolution of conflict, it served a vital function in that these were some of the very few people willing to investigate alternative methods. Many activists became some of the first to take the burgeoning ideas of conflict resolution to the public. Two groups rate a special mention in the growth of conflict resolution: Quakers and Mennonites. The Quakers' long-standing pacifism created the necessity to look for alternatives to conflict. Mennonites, in a similar vein to the Quakers, also sought the creation of alternatives. These two groups played key roles in advancing the language of conflict resolution.

Kenneth Boulding, himself a Quaker, was a key participant in the early conflict resolution movement. Boulding, Anatol Rapoport, Herbert Kelman, Quincy Wright and others joined forces in the mid-1950s in an attempt to examine the sources of conflict. In 1957 the *Journal of Conflict Resolution* (JCR) was first published, with Boulding taking a leading role. Harty and Modell (1991, p. 731) explain that the objective of those writing in the JCR was 'to develop a new general theory of the causes and prevention of all types of human conflict'. JCR founders further explained that their

> main concern is to stimulate a new approach, especially in the direction of the formulation and testing of theoretical models related to the central problem ... We are interested also in the improvement of the information processes in this area through quantification, index numbers, or any other means. (quoted in Harty and Modell, 1991, p. 731)

The JCR has acted as a substantial force in moving the study of conflict processes and conflict resolution forward. Yet it is limited in its appeal by its continued perpetuation of its founder's intentions to pursue a study of conflict through quantification (e.g. game theory). There are many who view this as antithetical to the effective study of conflict.

Perhaps more than any other historical intellectual component of conflict resolution, international relations and the peace movement added significantly to the understanding of human behaviour and the sources of conflict.

Alternative Dispute Resolution

At roughly the same time as the rise of the workshop movement and the changes in organizational development there surfaced an increase in dissatisfaction with the methods used to administer justice and resolve community disputes. Alternative dispute resolution (ADR) grew out of this dissatisfaction, and continues to grow. Generally, ADR concerns a set of procedures and processes designed to provide alternatives to adjudicated settlement of conflict. As Goldberg *et al.* point out, however, settling disputes prior to adjudication is nothing new:

> Even before there was an ADR movement, methods other than litigation were used for resolving disputes. Some claims were not 'voiced' at all for fear of alienating the offender, and those that were raised often were resolved by a host of indigenous mechanisms such as the ward boss, the village priest, and the family friends. (Goldberg *et al.*, 1992, p. 6)

What differentiates the ADR movement from those other alternative methods is simply the movement itself. Since the early 1980s there has been a rapidly growing trend, especially in the West, to institutionalize specialists in ADR techniques. Those specialists include conciliators, mediators, arbitrators and mini-trial judges. ADR techniques are often used in the context of court-annexed dispute resolution, where the courts use the ADR process to reduce the caseload of the court, or in an attempt to provide a better method for resolution.

For example, the Family Court in Australia, begun in 1975, is an early example of the employment of ADR techniques in trying to resolve the special problems of family conflict. Astor and Chinkin (1992, p. 7) explain:

> Before it [the Family Court] was established criticism had been addressed to problems with the court structure and the '... legalistic procedures

which face married couples should they turn to the law to resolve their interpersonal problems.' The new court was designed as a 'helping court' with active pre-divorce and post-divorce counselling facilities to assist reconciliation and to provide for the reduction of bitterness and distress and the alleviation of ongoing post-divorce problems.

The court uses a counselling model which in many ways is very reminiscent of mediation. Although the court has not surrendered its jurisdiction, it has provided other means by which disputes may be handled. ADR in general reflects the Australian Family Court process, in that nowhere has it replaced the legalistic model as such; ADR operates within the legalistic model, while at the same time recognizing shortcomings of the legal system.

Not all ADR has been directly linked to the courts. In 1976 the San Francisco Community Boards were founded. These were developed to provide citizens with an alternative to the traditional models of resolving neighbourhood disputes. ADR moves to develop community-based dispute resolution programmes continue to spread throughout the USA, and internationally too. In Australia, for example, are the Community Justice Centres, which opened in 1980 in Sydney and are funded by the New South Wales government. Neither the American nor the Australian example of community justice centres has, as yet, been proven to reduce the levels of neighbourhood conflict. Astor and Chinkin (1991), for example, assert that in San Francisco the Community Boards mediate only about 100 cases annually.

ADR has also branched out of traditional 'empowering' efforts, such as the Community Justice Centres and Community Boards, and moved into other, more specialized areas. For example, public disputes (such as environmental disputes) are more and more coming under the influence of ADR methods. Carpenter and Kennedy (1988) argue that ADR may be used in public disputes, which they describe as involving 'a wide range of complex issues. A controversy over toxic waste storage, for example, raises health and economic issues as well as the technical questions of how to construct and maintain facilities' (p. 9). In many ways, ADR is becoming an alternative method for policymaking, and now often travels under the title of 'reg-neg', or regulation/negotiation.

ADR has provided conflict resolution with an institutional framework. Although ADR does not engage in the far-reaching analysis of problems, like organizational development, it has informed much of the public discourse about conflict resolution. It has also faced the institutional problems that are faced by conflict resolution.

Conclusion: Trends and Currents in Conflict

The imperative to resolve conflict is clearly represented in the activities of many scholars and practitioners. While the imperative to resolve conflicts rests with scholars and practitioners, it is also worth considering some of the societal influences that constrain the resolution of conflict. Resolving conflict is not a value-free activity; indeed, as the name suggests, resolving conflict is held in high esteem over conflict continuance. The values that inform conflict resolution are largely Western, and may act to inhibit its useful application across cultural and political barriers. Western notions of conflict resolution include non-violence, fairness, individual choice and empowerment, and the support for a variety of fundamental principles (whether described as human rights, common sense or human needs).

The tradition of conflict resolution cannot be divorced from its day-to-day practice. Therefore, how conflict resolution accounts for and replies to social and structural constraints is largely dependent upon its past. Conflict resolution had three clear influences that have guided its development: management theory, international relations and alternative dispute resolution. The manner in which these schools have interacted with one another and society at large is reflected in many of the theoretical debates and contests that have been carried out. Later chapters will show clearly the degree to which the field of conflict resolution is divided. One area where this division in the field comes through is found in the definition of conflict.

In the next chapter the popular conceptions of conflict handling are considered. These popular conceptions underscore areas of agreement and difference between the public and academics. While there are many areas of disagreement and divergence in the field, it should be clear, however, that advances continue to be made.

References

Astor, Hilary and Christine M. Chinkin (1992) *Dispute Resolution in Australia*. Sydney: Butterworths.
Blake, Robert R. and Jane S. Mouton (1964) *The Managerial Grid*. Houston: Gulf Publishing.

Burton, John (1986) 'History of Conflict Resolution', in Linus Pauling (ed.), *World Encyclopedia of Peace*, vol. 1. Oxford: Pergamon Press.

Carpenter, Susan L. and W.J.D. Kennedy (1988) *Managing Public Disputes*. San Francisco: Jossey-Bass.

Follett, Mary Parker (1995) 'Constructive Conflict' (1925). Reprinted in *Mary Parker Follett: Prophet of Management*, ed. Pauline Graham. Boston: Harvard Business School Press.

Galbraith, John (1996) *The Good Society*. London: Sinclair-Stevenson.

Goldberg, Stephen B., Frank E.A. Sander and Nancy H. Rogers (1992) *Dispute Resolution*. Boston: Little, Brown and Co.

Harty, Martha and John Modell (1991) 'The First Conflict Resolution Movement, 1956–1971', *Journal of Conflict Resolution* 35(4), 720–58.

Hill, Barbara (1982) 'An Analysis of Conflict Resolution Techniques', *Journal of Conflict Resolution* 26(1), 109–38.

Mouzelis, Nicos P. (1981) *Organisation and Bureaucracy*. London: Routledge and Kegan Paul.

Pascale, Robert Tanner (1990) *Managing on the Edge*. New York: Touchstone Books.

Scimecca, Joseph (1991) 'Conflict Resolution in the United States: The Emergence of a Profession?', in Kevin Avruch, Peter Black and Joseph Scimecca (eds), *Conflict Resolution: Cross Cultural Perspectives*. New York: Greenwood.

Simon, Herbert (1957) *Models of Man*. New York: Wiley.

2
POPULAR CONCEPTIONS
OF HANDLING CONFLICT

Introduction

Not too surprisingly, the popular notion of conflict handling is rather different from the academic. The popular notion is fed by a variety of factors, including mass media, writers of popular texts and common experience. These three combine to forge a view of conflict handling that diverges sharply from the actual development of the field. This popular view, then, also feeds back into the academic discourse on the field and impacts on it in unpredicted ways. Popularized versions of conflict handling are even entering the world of fiction. For example, Michael Crichton's *Disclosure* contains a scene of 'mediation', albeit a poor representation. Increasingly, the public is coming to acknowledge and recognize the existence of conflict-handling mechanisms. The popular press is largely responsible for raising the profile of such terms as 'mediator'. It is also largely responsible for the poor understanding many members of the public have of the terms. Others, such as trade union members, are aware of terms such as mediation, arbitration and the like, but may also not understand precisely how they work, or what their objective is.

Conflict-handling Processes

Before we move on to examine how the popular mind is influenced over conflict handling it will be useful briefly to describe a variety of conflict-handling practices. There are a variety of views on what constitutes the practice of conflict handling or resolution. Schellenberg (1996), for example, identifies five basic practices in the resolution of conflict, including coercion, negotiation and bargaining, adjudication, mediation and arbitration. Burton and Dukes (1990) categorize all processes under three headings: management, settlement and resolution. Under each of those headings a variety of processes appear, as set out in Table 2.1. Goldberg *et al.* (1992), who identify four categories of process, including negotiation, mediation, arbitration and hybrid processes, reflect a more conservative approach.

It will be useful to outline here some definitions and provide descriptions of many of these processes. The major processes focused on here include negotiation, mediation, arbitration and adjudication.

The process of *negotiation* is well covered in both the popular and academic press. Thousands, if not millions, of words have been written on how to negotiate better, differently or more successfully. The *Negotiation Journal* is the centrepiece of academic study of negotiation and is published by the Harvard Negotiation Project. The academic literature focuses primarily on negotiation in managerial contexts, though some authors are expanding the range of coverage. Lewicki *et al.* (1994) and Pruitt and Carnevale (1993) have broadened the range of coverage in describing negotiation as a more generic social activity, not limited to the boardroom. Pruitt and Carnevale (1993, p. 2) define negotiation as 'a discussion between two or more parties with the apparent aim of resolving divergence of interest and thus escaping social conflict'. A central characteristic of negotiation is interdependence. Lewicki *et al.* (1994, p. 24) write, 'Interdependent relationships are characterised by interlocking goals – both parties need each other to accomplish their goals.'

Negotiations may be either formal or informal. Formal negotiations are typified by labour–management contract discussions, meetings between heads of state and performance appraisals, for example. Informal negotiations occur all the time, without the same levels of expectation and social definition. For instance, an

Table 2.1 Burton and Dukes's categorization of conflict-handling processes

Management	Settlement	Resolution
Mediation	Adjudication	Citizen diplomacy
Divorce mediation	Arbitration	T-group resolution
Victim–offender reconciliation	Ombudsmanry	Track two diplomacy
Community mediation		Problem-solving conflict resolution
Environmental and public policy mediation		Deductive analysis

informal negotiation may take place between a married couple over who will drive the children to school. In this example, the parties may not even recognize that they are in a negotiation, yet they still depend upon one another for an outcome, and they are both working towards resolving a divergence of interest between them.

Mediation is another method for handling conflict and is becoming an increasingly popular term in the discussion of conflict resolution. Folberg and Taylor (1984, p. 7) define mediation as 'the process by which the participants, together with the assistance of a neutral person or persons, systematically isolate disputed issues in order to develop options, consider alternatives, and reach consensual settlement that will accommodate their needs'. The definition of mediation is broad in its coverage and can incorporate a variety of different people in many different settings. Today mediators can be found in the legal profession, for example. Lawyers, trained as mediators, seek to resolve differences between their clients through the use of this informal process, in order to save court costs. Other places where mediation is found include labour–management relations, for example. The US Federal Mediation and Conciliation Service was established to provide mediation in labour–management disputes. Mediation is now used to facilitate the effective and smooth dissolution of marital contracts, reconcile criminal victims and offenders, address workplace disputes, handle workplace grievances and settle petty disputes in neighbourhoods.

Variations on mediation also exist. 'Med-arb' is a hybrid process, whereby a mediator seeks to facilitate agreement between parties, until such time as it is clear that the parties cannot reach an agreement. At that point the mediator 'switches hats' and takes on the role of arbitrator and imposes a solution on the parties. This hybrid process is most commonly used in labour–management disputes. Another variation on the mediation theme is conciliation. In the USA 'conciliation' and 'mediation' are used almost interchangeably, whereas elsewhere in the world 'conciliation' takes on a slightly different meaning. Rather than being a neutral third party, a conciliator is not neutral to the public good. Conciliators are used, for example, in Australia by the New South Wales Anti-Discrimination Board. The conciliator may be neutral in terms of the dispute between the parties, but is not neutral in terms of the relationship between the dispute and state and federal legislation. Conciliators often use much more directive language in an effort to lead parties to an agreement that upholds legislative dictates.

Within the mediation field there are a number of contested issues, including the nature of mediator power, neutrality and accreditation. Increasingly, mediators are becoming more professionalized and institutionalized. As this process continues it has real implications for the principle of a neutral mediator – after all, how can a mediator be neutral if the mediator is an employee of an organization? Presumably, the mediator is not neutral over his or her own self-interest, for instance.

Arbitration is another often-mentioned process in handling conflict. Goldberg *et al.* (1992) describe arbitration as often voluntary, final and binding. This means that in most arbitration settings the use of arbitration is up to the parties themselves, and its outcome is agreed by the parties to be the final word on the dispute. This is the ideal, but of course reality may lag somewhat. Arbitration has been used in a variety of commercial and labour–management contexts to resolve problems, rather than go to court. The process grows out of a legal environment, and so it reflects many of the characteristics of legal discourse. Not all arbitration is voluntary. In some instances contracts may stipulate the use of arbitration as the method of resolving problems. Indeed, in some legislative contexts, arbitration has been mandated as the method of addressing disputes and conflicts.

There are variations in the conduct of arbitration. For example, classical arbitration occurs when both parties present their cases in a similar fashion to two sides in a legal case. The arbitrator hears both sides, weighs up the merits of the two sides and crafts an outcome for the parties. Final-offer arbitration, however, differs markedly from the classical form. Final-offer arbitration occurs with both parties presenting a case. The arbitrator may pick only one of the two cases; he or she cannot deviate from what is presented. In classical arbitration the parties tend to overstate their cases, knowing that the arbitrator will base his or her solutions on what is heard. In final-offer arbitration, because the arbitrator can only choose the case presented by one or other party, this tends to force both parties to be reasonable, in case the other party is more reasonable.

Arbitration does nothing to address the underlying relationship between the parties. In this way it does nothing actually to resolve the conflict as such. It may resolve the outstanding issue between the party, but feelings of ill will and the like are left unaddressed.

Adjudication is the process with which most people are familiar. Many litigants use the courts in an effort to resolve disputes and conflicts between parties. Courts, however, are not designed to address relationship problems, but rather to resolve points of law. As such they may work very well through the adversarial system, but resolving points of law may not always provide solace in conflict situations. In fact, resolving an outstanding point of law may do nothing but exacerbate a conflict. The use of courts, however, is perhaps the most common institutional method employed in an effort to resolve conflicts and disputes. Ultimately, courts impose a settlement on the parties, who have no option but to accept the opinion of the court. In many ways the courts are deemed the final social stopping-point of many disputes and conflicts. Of course, the feelings and emotions that go with conflicts may not be resolved by a simple act of the court. Resolving these aspects of conflict has been deemed by many to be the province of mediation. Yet even there, mediation does not always accomplish its goal.

In consideration of any conflict-handling process it is useful to recognize the distinction between process and content. In negotiation, the parties must attend to the ways in which the negotiation is conducted, as well as to what is being said. In mediation, arbitration and adjudication the situation is a little different. Parties to the conflict take on greater responsibility for the content, leaving considerations of process to the third party. The mediator, arbitrator and judge become responsible for handling process. The distinction between process and content informs the majority of conflict-handling literature, though the lines are often blurred.

A key contributor to the development of the distinction between process and content originated from experiments conducted during the 1970s. Thibaut and Walker (1975) examined the relationship between process control and satisfaction. Their study revealed that parties who possessed a low level of process control perceived outcomes as less fair than those who possessed a high level of process control. The emphasis on process was the key for those studying conflict resolution. If an outcome is perceived as fair, it is more likely to 'work' in the long run than outcomes perceived as unfair. Therefore, giving parties a high degree of process control is important for successful conflict resolution. The great promise of both mediation and arbitration is that they afford participants greater process control than other forms of conflict-handling mechanisms.

Although process control, or procedural fairness as it is also known, is important to understanding how conflict handling processes work, other factors also have an impact. The popular conceptions of conflict handling also play a role.

The Mass Media and Conflict Handling

The popular mass media image of conflict resolution is an unfortunate one. The use of language and the description of role leads one to make some erroneous assumptions about the nature of conflict handling. For example, the USA is described as playing a mediating role in the Middle East between Israelis and Palestinians. Describing the US role as a mediating one should lead one to conclude that the USA is neutral towards the outcome between the parties. Yet the reality of US foreign policy is such that the USA is not neutral towards the parties. It has a variety of relationships with the Israelis that are very unlike relationships with the Palestinians. Such a state of affairs suggests that the USA is anything but neutral towards the outcome of negotiations between the Israelis and Palestinians.

Rather than playing a mediating role in the Middle East, the USA is playing a coercive one, albeit while trying to maintain a positive public image. The same can be said of the US role in Northern Ireland and other points of conflict in the world. This is not a problem that is exclusive to the USA. Rather, it is in the nature of international relations; no nation can or will be totally neutral in an international negotiation. International mediation cannot be conducted under the auspices of a single nation-state. Rather, international mediation is more likely to occur when conducted by either the United Nations or a non-governmental organization (NGO), or a coalition of nations.

The mass media tend to accept others' descriptions of their actions rather uncritically. If a party defines itself as a mediator, then the press tends to accept that description. In part this stems from a lack of understanding on the part of the press, and it may also have do with issues of journalist training and ethics. Whatever its cause, however, it has ramifications on how the public understand and discuss conflict handling.

Popular Texts

A major source of interest in conflict handling has come from a number of popular texts on the subject of conflict. There are several that are worth mentioning, including *Getting to Yes*, by Roger Fisher, William Ury and Bruce Paton (1991); *Beyond Machiavelli* by Roger Fisher, Elizabeth Kopelman and Andrea Kupfer Schneider (1994) and *Conflicts* by Edward De Bono (1985). Each one of these has had commercial success, and each has contributed to the public understanding of conflict handling. Each has also had a negative impact, in that these books have established certain beliefs about the nature of conflict that are not well reflected in the academic literature and do not necessarily reflect the true nature of conflict. These popular texts tend to suffer from the same three criticisms: they trivialize conflict, routinize methods of handling conflict, and undervalue the role that situation and context play in handling conflict.

There is a tremendous tendency to trivialize conflict in popular texts. Nowhere is this trivialization more obvious than in how these authors consider emotions. People in conflict are often angry, often motivated by extreme emotions such as hate. Yet consider the view of Fisher *et al.* (1991, p. 29): 'In a negotiation, particularly a bitter dispute, feelings may be more important than talk.' In conflict, emotions are as important as, if not always more important than, what the authors refer to as talk. Fisher *et al.* (1991) provide several suggestions in dealing with opponents' emotions, such as 'recognize and understand emotions', 'make emotions explicit and legitimate', 'permit parties to ventilate emotions', and 'avoid reacting to emotional outbursts'. Not only does the language trivialize emotion, but the suggested behaviour does as well. Imagine allowing a victim of the Holocaust to ventilate emotion – the emotional pain caused by the Holocaust is still being ventilated and one suspects it will be for some centuries to come. The emotional pain caused by the death of six million Jews cannot be easily ventilated.

De Bono's (1985) message also trivialized conflict. While he recognizes the role that emotion plays in conflict, he places the responsibility for resolving conflict on one party's shoulders. Essentially, De Bono's point is that if you change the way you think about conflict and resolving conflict, then the outcome you obtain will be different. If only life were that simple – but unfortunately it is not. Changing thought patterns, styles and methods is not easy; societies have built up impressive lists of failed attempts at changing thinking. Anti-racist campaigns are, more often than not, failures, for example. De Bono's optimism may be pleasant to read, but is most improbable in the real world.

Perhaps most worrisome of all is the emphasis on win–win outcomes, or simply agreements that generate mutual gain. While it may be easy as an outsider to invent solutions that provide mutual payoffs to two parties, the parties themselves may not see it that way. What was the mutual gain agreement that would have left apartheid in place? For a black African it is unclear what this would

have been. For some conflict there simply is no way to create a
mutual gain; one side may have to 'win', while the other 'loses'. The
question may be more how to design an agreement that leaves open
the possibility for building relationships in the future. Yet to glibly
term that kind of tough situation win–win or even mutual benefit is
to make the situation appear trivial.

One of the keys to the commercial success of these texts has been
to routinize the handling of conflict. The title to Weeks's (1992)
book, *The Eight Essential Steps to Conflict Resolution*, is perhaps an
indicator of a most worrisome trend. The obvious question is why
eight steps and not seven, or nine. The desire to derive simple
models seems overwhelming. It appears commercially attractive to
develop one method that can be applied to a whole host of
situations.

Take the 'principled negotiation' of Fisher *et al.* (1991). The
authors describe a principled negotiation as one informed by
separating people from the problem, focusing on interests rather than
positions, designing options for mutual payoff, and emphasizing the
use of objective criteria by which to measure the negotiation. It is
easy to critique these four principles. It may be impossible to separate
the person from the problem because the problem may be the person.
Focusing on interests rather than positions is no guarantee that
matters will be made any easier; things may get worse when focusing
on the underlying interests to the negotiation. Designing options for
mutual payoffs may not be practical; even though parties creatively
generate options, reality may prevent the implementation of creative
solutions. Finally, objective criteria may not be available, especially if
one is dealing with highly subjective matters such as feeling.

Given that these four principles may not work, one must ask how
they are to be implemented across the range of possible conflicts.
They may work in a limited number of situations, but it would be
counterproductive to ask parties in conflict to behave in such a
routine manner. Instead, it might prove more useful to have parties
think critically about their situation and design steps more
appropriate to their needs.

Finally, these popular texts tend to undervalue context and
situation in conflict. Fisher *et al.* (1994) focus much of their attention
on perception and how parties see the conflict. Although this is
admirable, there is an emphasis upon persuasion, in an effort to
change views. To put it another way, the authors emphasize focusing
on what parties say about their conflict, not in order to understand
the conflict situation, but rather as a tool for persuasion. This is

unfortunate. For these authors the situation appears unimportant in its detail, but important only to persuade parties out of their conflicts. Barbarity, violence and pestilence, then, become not detail of the conflict, but rather mere points for persuasion. Poverty in Haiti, rather than being the basis for conflict, simply becomes an interesting point for the persuasive negotiator.

In sum, these sorts of approaches, though popular and publicly accessible, do nothing to contribute to an understanding of the dynamics of conflict. Rather they serve to skew the public debate and discussion over the nature of conflict and how to handle it. Cope and Kalantzis (1997, p. 280) addressing workplace conflict, comment:

> In the world where large corporate cultures and small teams are supposed to express shared values, win–win conflict resolution strategies are frequently applied. We can get together and resolve our differences, it is supposed, and everyone should come out winners. This, in reality, is a cultural discourse, not a neutral one. This is the discourse of nice guy liberalism, the passive–aggressive discourse of politeness, the patronising discourse of trying to get what you want while trying to tell somebody else that they are getting what they should want. Some people play this discourse better than others. The win–win discourse expresses superficial niceness while papering over differences and creating sublimated frustration. When people differ, the outcomes will almost invariably be asymmetrical, variations on win–lose or degrees of lose–lose. Indeed, agreeing to differ may be the optimal outcome, even the most productive one. The best negotiation will not be forced to end with win–win.

Generalized across all conflict contexts, the win–win discourse is not one of genuine conflict resolution, but rather a mechanism for persuading others that they have what they want, without really giving anything away. It is clever, but not very productive towards long-term resolution of conflict.

Common Experience

The experience of parties in conflict handling has also affected the way in which we understand and talk about conflict handling. Individuals who experience conciliation, mediation or other processes talk about and discuss them rather uncritically. As in the media, if somebody describes himself or herself as a mediator, then that is what they are, regardless of what they actually did. The public becomes bombarded with a confusing morass of often self-serving rhetoric that upon analysis ends up being wrong. For example, there are already a variety of compulsory mediations occurring in the world. Yet a central tenet of mediation is that it is voluntary, and making it compulsory changes the dynamics significantly. When parties go through compulsory mediation, they report the experience as mediation, and not something else. That experience, then, becomes superimposed on other situations. In a world of court-annexed mediation, mediation is no longer voluntary but compulsory.

These common experiences tend to skew and alter public perception of the nature of conflict handling. Mediators may be hired to resolve disputes in the workplace, for example, and then meet parties who insist that the mediator arbitrate! This kind of behaviour is not unexpected in a world where an uncritical perspective is taken on conflict handling.

Even the supposed benefits of a process such as mediation are repeated in wooden, mantra-like succession. Mediation, according to the popular wisdom, is supposed to be efficient, empowering and cheap. Yet the evidence that supports these contentions is mixed, at best. Still, the public are bombarded by these claims and come to believe them, and are then surprised when their mediation is expensive and time-consuming, and they feel no more empowered than before.

Conclusion

The world of conflict handling is filled with many different forces. Different people have spent whole lifetimes trying to describe and understand the process of conflict. Karl Marx, for example, spent years trying to understand the sources of and impact of class conflict. Yet some writers seem able to find the answers to conflict with little or no trouble. Writers who trivialize, routinize and underestimate conflict do nothing towards its resolution. In fact, such popularizations may do more to create conflict than otherwise. By falsely lifting expectations, the popular view of how to best deal with conflict may actually create the seeds of heightening conflict. After employing the popular methods of conflict resolution, some parties may become disheartened and instead opt for violence.

A more textured and refined understanding of conflict handling is required in order that better choices may be made concerning its ultimate resolution. In the chapters that follow, attention will be paid to a variety of forces that impinge upon conflict handling. By accounting for these forces, conflict may be better handled and perhaps even ultimately resolved. In the next chapter the focus turns to definitions and meanings: what is conflict and where does it come from?

References

Burton, John and Frank Dukes (1990) *Conflict: Practices in Management, Settlement and Resolution*. New York: St Martin's Press.

Cope, Bill and Mary Kalantzis (1997) *Productive Diversity*. Annandale, Australia: Pluto Press.

De Bono, Edward (1985) *Conflicts*. Harmondsworth: Penguin Books.

Fisher, Roger, Elizabeth Kopelman and Andrea Kupfer Schneider (1994) *Beyond Machiavelli*. Cambridge, MA: Harvard University Press.

Fisher, Roger, William Ury and Bruce Paton (1991) *Getting to Yes*. Harmondsworth: Penguin Books.

Folberg, Jay and Alison Taylor (1984) *Mediation*. San Francisco: Jossey-Bass.

Goldberg, Stephen B., Frank E.A. Sander and Nancy H. Rogers (1992) *Dispute Resolution*. Boston: Little, Brown and Co.

Lewicki, Roy J., Joseph A. Litterer, John W. Minton and David M. Saunders (1994) *Negotiation*. Burr Ridge, IL: Irwin.

Pruitt, Dean G. and Peter J. Carnevale (1993) *Negotiation in Social Conflict*. Buckingham: Open University Press.

Schellenberg, James A. (1996) *Conflict Resolution*. Albany: State University of New York Press.

Thibaut, J. and L. Walker (1975) *Procedural Justice: A Psychological Analysis*. Hillsdale, NJ: Lawrence Erlbaum.

Weeks, Dudley (1992) *The Eight Essential Steps to Conflict Resolution*. Los Angeles: Jeremy P. Tarcher.

3
ASSUMPTIONS AND MEANINGS IN CONFLICT RESOLUTION

How human nature and its impact upon conflict are understood carries profound implications for how conflict is handled. Embedded within each account of conflict are sets of assumptions on the nature of human action and motivation. Three perspectives or sets of assumptions on the origins of human behaviour include inherency, contingency and the interactionist perspective. The inherency perspective holds that human behaviour comes from within the individual, and is probably genetic in kind. The contingency perspective holds that human behaviour is a by-product of human intercourse, or socialization. Finally, the interactionist perspective sees human behaviour as an interaction between inherent human characteristics and the social environment. Before examining these topics, however, it will be useful to define conflict.

What Is Conflict?

Conflict is a term used to mean a variety of things, in an assortment of contexts. Under the mantle of conflict are words such as fight, argue, contest, debate, combat, war, and other equally evocative terms. One of the key problems in studying conflict is to know which descriptions of behaviour fit under the title of conflict. A useful starting-point is the scope of meaning of conflict. Does physical aggression equate with verbal aggression? Is an ongoing verbal 'conflict' within the workplace somehow comparable to military combat? How one answers these questions has considerable bearing on what kind of evidence can be brought to bear in understanding human interaction. If, for example, all warfare is excluded from the study of conflict resolution, then there is much in military history that must also be excluded from the study of conflict resolution. Equally, if it is argued that conflict concerns only events where physical resources are expended, such as in warfare, then a whole range of material may have to be excluded from consideration, especially psychology, communication studies and even anthropology.

Definitions of conflict fall into two groups. First, there are those that define conflict as largely subjective and focus on the individual. A second set places an emphasis on the external and objective qualities of conflict, thus emphasizing the social and overt behavioural aspects of conflict. Morton Deutsch emphasizes the subjective nature of conflict, writing:

> the presence or absence of conflict is never rigidly determined by the objective state of affairs. Apart from the possibility of misperception, psychological factors enter into the determination of conflict in yet another crucial way. Conflict is also determined by what is valued by the conflicting parties. Even the classical example of pure conflict – two starving men on a lifeboat with only enough food for the survival of one – loses its impact if one or both of the men have social or religious values that can become more dominant psychologically than the hunger need or the desire for survival.
>
> The point of these remarks is that neither the occurrence nor the outcome of conflict is completely and rigidly determined by objective circumstances. (Deutsch, 1973, p. 11)

From an objectivist perspective, conflict may be defined as a phenomenon that occurs when one or more parties perceive incompatible goals and then equally perceive interference from the other in their desire to obtain their goal. Yet it is not that Muslims and Christians perceive incompatible goals; it is the fact that they believe that the existence of the other's behaviour will interfere in their own goal attainment that leads to conflict. Furthermore, conflict, unlike the tango, does not require a minimum of two people: only one person need perceive conflict in order that it may exist. With this definition in mind, then, we can see that conflict types exist on a continuum where at one end is simple argumentation and at the other is total warfare. As one moves up the continuum there is a corresponding increase in the expenditure of resources and social organization.

The objectivist definition is broad, incorporating a wide range of human behaviour. Such a wide scope of definition may, however, create difficulty. One example of the difficulty in adopting such broad definitions is found in Galtung's definition of structural violence. Galtung (1990, p. 10) has defined structural violence as 'that which increases the distance between the potential and the actual, and that which impedes the decrease of this distance'. Thus, if somebody dies of starvation when food was present, then that person died violently if food had been withheld. One of the many criticisms offered against such a broad definition of violence is that it dilutes the true impact of physical violence. Where the word starvation is quite adequate to refer to death from hunger, why replace it with structural violence? There is merit to this line of questioning. An equivalent criticism may be raised against a broad definition of conflict. Why call warfare conflict, thus equating it with a feud in the office, when warfare will suffice to describe the expenditure of physical, political, cultural and psychic resources in an effort to kill one's opponent? Again, there is merit in this criticism; yet there is another side. Battlefield violence and workplace struggles share many similarities. Parties organize for fighting, and expend resources, engage in propaganda campaigns and take prisoners. There is territory to be won, both following battle and at the end of a planning meeting. These are not mere flights of linguistic metaphor, but rather reflect the profound ways in which the lessons learned from one conflict are easily transferred along, both up and down, the continuum and applied elsewhere.

One must recognize that the way in which one defines conflict will have a considerable impact on the way in which conflict resolution is carried out. For example, if conflict is defined as inevitable, then there may be no reason even to try to resolve it. Kriesberg (1982) has argued that theories of conflict may be divided into three general groups: those that view conflict as 'relations between different categories or groups'; those that view it as being primarily interpersonal; and those that see it as being largely found in institutions and social structures. This perspective represents a rather traditional way of dividing the conflict pie: interpersonal, group and social. It is not the only way in which one can examine conflict, however.

A more helpful way of seeing conflict is to divide theories into those which are largely functional – holding that conflict serves a social function; those that view it as situational – finding expression under certain situations; and those who hold it to be largely interactive. Perhaps another way to say this is that the functionalists ask the question 'Why is there conflict? What purpose does it serve?'

Situationalists ask, 'When do we have conflict? Under what circumstances does it occur?' Interactionists inquire as to 'How is there conflict? What methods and mechanisms are used to express it?'

Most noteworthy in the functionalist school was Georg Simmel, the German sociologist. Simmel, arguably one of the most influential writers on conflict, defined conflict as that which is 'designed to resolve divergent dualisms; it is a way of achieving some kind of unity, even if it be through the annihilation of one of the conflicting parties' (1955, p. 13). To Simmel, conflict served a social purpose, in that it reconciled contending forces. Reconciliation, in Simmel's terms, came even with the total destruction of one party. Simmel can be criticized, however, in that he sees conflict in teleological terms – as existing to serve some specific purpose.

Picking up this concept of functionality, Lewis Coser, an American sociologist and author of *The Functions of Social Conflict* (1957), defined conflict as 'the clash of values and interests, the tension between what is and what some groups feel ought to be' (p. 197). For Coser, conflict served the function of pushing society onward, of leading to new institutions, technology and economic systems. If social 'progress' is built upon new solutions to problems, then conflict becomes a required precursor to that change. Therefore, a society without conflict is a dead society. Of course, one could inquire as to whether progress really did come from new answers to problems, and whether conflict was the only way to generate those new answers. Furthermore, the meaning of progress could equally be challenged. What, exactly, constitutes progress?

In a different vein other scholars have defined conflict in less functional terms. Bercovitch (1984), a situationalist, for example, defines conflict as a 'situation which generates incompatible goals or values among different parties' (p. 6). For Bercovitch, conflict is situation dependent; it is the situation which calls into question whether conflict exists. While conflict does not serve a purpose as such, it does arise because of given conditions (either social or personal) which bring into play 'incompatibility'. This suggests, then, that there is something about a given situation that is different from another situation. So, there may be two situations where the parties may be identical, even the issues, but since the situations vary (time, place, other parties) the outcome is different: one is conflictual and the other pacific. Although Bercovitch acknowledges the influence of the persons in conflict, he also argues that external factors must also impact on conflict behaviour. Bercovitch's approach to conflict echoes that of Galtung's concept of structural violence, where systemic structures, acting to reduce what one could have had, are seen to act as if they were violent; they are said to be structurally violent. Galtung's concept of structural violence is a situational perspective of conflict. As Galtung (1990, p. 10) writes, 'A life expectancy of only thirty years during the neolithic period was not an expression of violence, but the same life expectancy today (whether due to wars, or social injustice, or both) would be seen as violence according to our definition.' Thus for Galtung, it is the situation which is all-important; different situations are seen through varying lenses.

A step removed from Bercovitch and the situationalists are the communication interactionists. Folger *et al.* (1993, p. 4) define conflict as 'the interaction of interdependent people who perceive incompatible goals and interference from each other in achieving those goals'. These authors introduce two important concepts: interdependence and perception. Interdependence refers to those situations where one party's future actions are dependent upon another party's actions, and vice versa. Another key concept that they raised emphasizes perception as the key to bringing about conflict. As Tillett (1991, p. 8) points out, 'Conflict does not only come about when values or needs are actually, objectively incompatible, or when conflict is manifested in action; it exists when one of the parties *perceives* it to exist [emphasis original].' One party may perceive conflict, and yet there may be no external evidence that such an event is occurring. This perspective is perhaps best thought of as the interactionist communication perspective. Folger *et al.* see conflict as coming from interdependent people; that is, from those whose payoffs depend upon one another. There are problems with this notion of interdependence, especially when one considers conflicts that exist between parties who do not interact, do not share resources and generally are far apart. Such a conflict might exist between a small fascist cell in the Rocky Mountains in the USA and members of the Israeli Knesset. Neither party relies upon the other at all; one party may be only marginally aware of the existence of the other. Yet conflict still exists.

Regardless of the problems raised by the definition put forward by Folger *et al.*, they have managed to remove many of the functionalist aspects to conflict, but in doing so raise an important question. To what extent can conflict be seen as objective or subjective?

The objectivists hold that there are certain events, behaviours or situations that will create conflict. They would further argue that regardless of what people might think, if these conditions exist, then conflict must exist. Class theorists of conflict are objectivists, and perhaps the most notable of these is Marx. Provided there are class divisions, then regardless of what individuals think, there will be conflict between the lower-order class members and the higher-order class members. Those in the lower strata will seek to acquire power, while those in the higher order will be seeking to protect their power. Marx argued that those who are objectively in conflict, yet who express no knowledge of that conflict, are in a state of false consciousness. That is, they falsely believe, usually through propaganda from the ruling class, that there is no conflict. So, from a Marxist perspective, the working-class person who says that it is simply his or her lot in life to engage in difficult physical labour is suffering from false consciousness.

There are several difficulties, however, with the objectivist school. Not surprisingly, it is difficult to develop a clear picture of the objective conditions of conflict. One method for uncovering the existence of conflict is to ask people whether they are in conflict. If one asks a population whether they are in conflict, and they say no, then one faces a dilemma. One can postulate that regardless of what they say, they are in conflict, yet the question arises for the researcher, 'How do you know?' Furthermore, if the researcher then argues that poverty, for example, is an illustration of conflict, one still must explain why conflict, and not some other social phenomenon, has caused poverty, or grows out of poverty.

Against the objectivist school of conflict is the subjectivist school. For the subjectivists, conflict is in the perceptions of the parties in conflict. Using a parallel example of the objectivist conflict, an individual in an egalitarian society, who shares equal access to social institutions and who possesses a reasonable standard of living, may still perceive themselves to be in conflict with other members of society. The fact that the society is egalitarian does nothing to alter the internal state of the individual; that person still perceives himself or herself to be in conflict.

Once again we return to the problem faced by the researcher. In order to measure, or simply acquire knowledge about, conflict, one is totally reliant upon the opinions of the parties in conflict. So, the researcher is a captive of the moment, in that parties undergoing investigation may report at one moment that they are in conflict, and at another moment that they are not in conflict. Thus a totally subjective definition of conflict creates difficulties for the researcher,

though the fact of its being subjective ought not be the basis upon
which we either reject or accept it.

Underlying all views of conflict are values – how one views
conflict depends largely upon the values held. If, for example, you are
deeply motivated by a sense of justice, then conflict for you may be
seen in more objective terms. On the other hand, you may view
conflict as not necessarily related to justice, and see conflict as
sometimes beneficial. If this is the case, then you may define conflict
in more subjective terms. Thomas Schelling, in *The Strategy of Conflict*
(1980, p. 3) notes that

> Among the diverse theories of conflict – corresponding to the diverse
> meanings of the word 'conflict' – a main dividing line is between those
> that treat conflict as a pathological state and seek its causes and
> treatment, and those that take conflict for granted and study the
> behavior associated with it.

The manner in which you interpret the value of conflict will have a
great impact on the way you study conflict, but will also influence
the way in which you may or may not seek to resolve it.

Conflict and Time

No matter whether one takes an objectivist or subjectivist view of
conflict, time plays an important role in conflict. In 1651 Thomas
Hobbes (1974, p. 143), in *Leviathan*, observed:

> For WAR, consisteth not in battle only, or the act of fighting; but in a
> tract of time, wherein the will to contend by battle is sufficiently known;
> and therefore the notion of *time*, is to be considered in the nature of war;
> as it is in the nature of weather. For as the nature of foul weather, lieth
> not in a shower or two of rain; but in an inclination thereto of many days
> together: so the nature of war, consisteth not in actual fighting; but in
> the known disposition thereto, during all the time there is no assurance
> to the contrary. All other time is PEACE. [emphasis original]

Conflict in the office, as much as warfare, occurs over time. The fact
that it is not episodic is one of the central problems in trying to
handle conflict. Conflict consists in a set of issues or events that
persist to be important over time. Lewin argues that time perspective
plays an important part in the actions of people. He writes, 'Actions,
emotions, and certainly the morale of an individual at any instant
depend upon his total time perspective' (Lewin, 1997, p. 80). Conflict

is a historical process, and focused on the past. People in conflict have past orientation, and are often concerned with past injustices or events that led to present-day conditions. Not surprisingly, then, conflict resolution is concerned with actions today that will lead to a positive future.

Societal, Structural and Deep-rooted Conflict

There is a growing recognition of different varieties of conflict. The above definitions of conflict have, hopefully, steered us towards considering the more difficult end of the conflict spectrum. Thorson (1989, p. 2), in his introduction to *Intractable Conflicts and Their Transformation*, makes an important distinction:

> it is useful to think of two broad sorts of conflicts. The first, about which much is known, includes those conflicts in which the parties have, for whatever reasons, failed to recognize that some sort of efficient solution exists. A well-worn example of such a conflict is that between two children trying to divide up one cake. The classic solution has a parent suggest that one of the children divide the cake and then the other child select the first piece. This sort of solution has much appeal because it provides a way out of the dispute that will benefit each party. But disputes of this sort are inefficient precisely because there does exist a resolution that leaves such disputant in a better position than it was prior to the dispute. ...
>
> ...
>
> Not all conflicts are of this first type. For the cake division illustration to work, several background assumptions seem required. For instance, the illustration, as presented, is ahistorical. Nothing is said about prior interactions among the children. ...
>
> ...
>
> Likewise, it is assumed that the mechanism of resolution is separable from the conflict. In other words, the mechanism of resolution is simply a technical means for achieving a resolution and is itself not a part of the conflict. But what if something like self-determination is a part of the issue?

Rather than recognize a continuum as suggested above, Thorson recognizes a two-tier typology and notes that not all conflicts are easy. Not all are susceptible to traditional, or even alternative, dispute resolution methods. Each conflict is different in ways unique to itself. In Burton's schema the simple cake-like conflicts are better termed disputes, in that the problem can be solved by negotiating over interests. On the other hand, others would call the latter 'intractable' or deep-rooted conflicts in order to distinguish them from the cake-like conflicts. Thorson defines intractable conflicts as those which cannot be resolved. Burton (1987, p. 3) defines deep-rooted conflicts as those

> which involve deep feelings, values and needs [that] cannot be settled by an order from outside authority, such as a court, an arbitrator or a more powerful nation. These are conflicts which appear endless, erupting into emotional displays and even violence from time to time.

Whether they are 'deep rooted' or 'intractable', examples of such emotive conflicts include the Arab–Israeli conflict, Northern Ireland, US race relations, Muslim–Hindu conflict in India, and so on. These conflicts cannot be resolved by splitting the socio-economic pie differently, nor can they be resolved by goodwill, commitments to non-violence, goodness, or any other individual solution. Their resolution demands something different.

Unlike many modes of dealing with conflict, as exemplified by the courts, for example, deep-rooted, societal conflict demands the use of analytic tools. Conflict settlement concerns itself primarily with allocation of responsibility, and conflict management focuses on making conflict functional. The management of conflict requires a level of analysis, but analysis need only go so far as is absolutely required in making the level and intensity of conflict acceptable to the parties involved. So, for example, a settlement occurs when conflict that has erupted in domestic violence is settled by the court's handing down a ruling, and allocating blame. Those seeking to manage conflict, however, attempt to identify some of the immediate causes to the conflict (domestic violence in this case) and determine some method of amelioration. The level of amelioration sought goes only as far as is necessary for the parties to cope with the result. So, a forced separation and judicial order (such as a bench warrant) keeping the parties apart may be deemed sufficient to manage the conflict.

Unlike conflict settlement and management, conflict resolution requires a level of intellectual rigour not usually found in most efforts to address conflict. In his seminal work on conflict, *Fights, Games and Debates*, Anatol Rapoport writes, 'The task ... will be to examine not conflicts for their own interest but rather *different kinds of intellectual tools for the analysis of conflict situations*' (Rapoport, 1960, p. 12; emphasis original). He went on to add that 'no single framework of thought is adequate for dealing with such a complex class of phenomena as human conflict' (ibid., p. 359). Rapoport's conflict analyst is one who is a generalist, and who draws on a wide range of intellectual tools and traditions which will lead to the resolution of conflict.

In opposition to Rapoport's emphasis on the breadth of intellectual tools is, once again, the work of John Burton. Burton argues that conflict resolution must be informed by one intellectual framework, and that a reliance upon pragmatism leads only to the failure of conflict resolution. Burton and Dukes (1990, pp. 20–1) argue:

> If one is lost in a forest, trial and error could be a useful procedure. But trial and error applied to dispute or conflict situations, in which the quality of life and life itself may be at stake, is unacceptable.

To Burton's way of thinking, reliance on a single framework augurs against the likelihood of inappropriate and unworkable conflict resolution processes being adopted.

Many agree with Rapoport, however, regarding the breadth of analytical requirements for examining conflict. Burton's emphasis on a single framework is perhaps excessive. If a researcher were indeed simply employing trial and error, then perhaps his point would be valid, but it is unlikely that any researcher would behave in such a way. It is often seductive for the researcher in conflict to remove himself or herself from the very visceral and tangible nature of conflict. Rapoport is probably correct in his assessment that there is no one intellectual tool or framework from which conflict can be analysed and resolved. Burton's search for the right theory to unlock all conflicts simply does not appear likely to undo deep-rooted conflicts. For conflicts to become deep rooted they have usually persisted for a considerable amount of time and undergone considerable development. While it is certainly possible to find one theory which, given enough time, would undo such deep-rooted conflicts, it does not seem likely that such a theory would eventuate. But Rapoport falls down, too, in his inability to provide a clear-cut set of intellectual guides which the researcher can use in developing a set of theoretical tools to resolve deep-rooted conflict.

It is noteworthy that deep-rooted or intractable conflicts need not be limited to the societal level. There are, of course, deep-rooted and intractable interpersonal conflicts too. Yet there is a key distinction here: social and structural conflicts, intractable or otherwise, carry with them some fundamental differences from interpersonal conflicts. Most significantly, the scope of the conflict is simply different – if for no other reason than the fact that societal conflict can call on such a vast array of resources. There is room to argue that societal conflict and interpersonal conflict share many similar characteristics. This is true, but it is insufficient to say, then, that because they share some similarities, they ought to be conceptually joined together. Although interpersonal and societal conflicts share some similar characteristics of power, intensity and durability, and may even be cross-generational, they also possess some key differences.

Unexpectedly, cockroaches may explain one key difference between interpersonal and group conflicts. Baron *et al.* (1992) report on experiments conducted by Zajonc *et al.* in the 1960s examining the performance of cockroaches with and without an audience. The experimenters tested the speed with which cockroaches ran away from light, both in the presence of a cockroach audience, and alone. They discovered that cockroaches escaped more quickly from the light if there was a roach audience. From this experiment and others there has grown a body of literature examining the process of social facilitation, or how the social setting influences and facilitates behaviour. There are divergent views on whether there is indeed a social facilitation effect, but there can be no doubt that people behave differently in the presence of others, and within a group. People are aroused in different ways when in a group than when they are alone. This behavioural difference is one of the key starting-points for separating social conflict from interpersonal conflict. Some other differences include:

- Social conflict is, by definition, broader in scope.
- Social conflict has greater complexity because of its greater scope.
- While both interpersonal and societal conflict can be said to possess cultures of conflict, societal conflict carries with it a greater likelihood of institutional involvement.

The role of institutions in social conflicts carries with it considerable weight and influence. Institutions that administer justice, for example, carry with them a high degree of legitimacy and are viewed by many as absolutely critical to the functioning of any society. Institutions, though, do not move easily, they are not altered with great ease, and so become important players in the process of resolving social conflict. While institutions do play a key role in other kinds of conflict (e.g. interpersonal), their role is not central as in social conflict. In assessing a conflict situation a vital first step is uncovering the dynamics and analysing social conflict.

Perhaps the most crucial component in resolving conflict is analysis. All societal/structural conflict shares the common need for analysis as a precursor to resolution. The frameworks of analysis vary with different theoretical approaches. Burton is unique among conflict theorists in that he has posited a framework that, he argues, explains all conflict. Yet it seems clear that over-reliance on a single framework may unnecessarily limit the examination of the sources of conflict.

Theory Types: The Origins of Conflict

What are the sources of conflict? Are human beings destined always to experience conflict? Or is conflict something that can be eradicated? These are the basic questions that need to be addressed when examining structural and societal conflicts. How these questions are answered will influence the manner in which we attempt to resolve conflicts, or even whether we attempt conflict resolution. There are three basic theory types which must be considered. These types are inherency, contingency and interactionist.

A simple illustration of the schools of thought might be in order. The view that conflict is inherent has been expounded for centuries, if not millennia. One could argue that the story of Adam and Eve and the 'fall' is one of *inherency* – it was in the nature of humans to fall from paradise; it was inevitable. Eve, so the inherency argument goes, was destined to err. Her tasting of the forbidden fruit was not a matter of her exercise of free will, but rather, fundamental to her being. Thus there was nothing that could have been done to prevent the fall from paradise.

Unlike the inherency school, however, the *contingent* school would see the story of Adam and Eve differently. Eve's taking of the apple resulted from some external factors, outside of her being. She was tempted by the serpent, and persuaded to do something that she might not have done in other circumstances. Conditions apart from herself created powerful forces upon her behaviour, leading her to act as she did. Eve was not destined to err, but rather led to it. The fall from paradise, from the contingency perspective, was wholly preventable.

Different still from the inherency or contingency school is the *interactionist* view that behaviour depends upon both inherent and contingent factors, the two of which cannot be separated or further reduced. From this perspective Eve's behaviour depended upon both her biological self – the speed at which she acted, her innate intelligence, and the rest of her genetic make-up – and the external factors she found herself faced with, such as the power being exercised on her, her social situation and her status. Together, these forces combined to impact upon her and informed her behaviour.

The division between inherent, contingent and interactionist theories is not the only way to divide the 'theory world' into conceptual pieces. Kenneth Waltz (1959), for example, in *Man, the State, and War*, divided theories of human action into the First Image, or the biological and individual impulses; the Second Image, or the behaviour of nations; and the Third Image, or the behaviour of the international system. Waltz's perspective suffers, however, from the fact that it is largely descriptive and divides theories by their intended focus, as opposed to their conceptual make-up.

It will be useful to turn more fully, now, to examine some of the major theories that have been expounded in these areas. This is certainly not a complete canvassing of all the major theorists, but it serves as a useful overview. Many of the theories brought up under either category reflect the long-standing 'nature versus nurture' debate: the debate as to whether human behaviour is primarily affected by genes, or by social interactions.

Inherency Theories

A useful place to begin is with the work of Thomas Hobbes. Hobbes (1974) made the observation that humanity is characterized by ceaseless, and indeed relentless, thirst for power. For Hobbes, humans carry within them the inherent drive to fight, which demands that societies be led by power. Only by imposing will upon the ruled can society be organized to run efficiently and peacefully. Hobbes was followed some years later by the British rhetorician and politician Edmund Burke, who also saw humanity as inherently conflictual. Like Hobbes, Burke argued that the only way to curtail humanity's urge to conflict and violence is through law and custom. The writings of these British political philosophers influenced greatly the development of the democratic liberal state in the West.

One of the most influential forces in the inherency school was Sigmund Freud and his school of psychoanalysis. Fundamental to Freud's view of humanity are the contending life and death instincts. The life instinct has within it the desire for pleasure. The libido refers to the life energy within humans, though it was originally viewed by Freud as being reflected in terms of sexual energy. Opposed to the life instinct is the death instinct, or 'thanatos'. Freud (1990, p. 164) believed that thanatos 'turns into the destructive instinct when it is directed outwards on to objects'. The death instinct, however, can be transformed within the person to serve the purposes of life. Making the matter even more complex, the externalization of the death instinct, in the form of aggression, may be beneficial for the person, though harmful for those around.

It is worth spending just a little more time on this point. Hall (1954, p. 100) explains the Freudian concept: 'By taking aggressive action a person protects himself from being injured or destroyed by his enemies. Aggression also helps him to overcome barriers that stand in his way of the satisfaction of his basic needs.' By focusing the death instinct away from the organism, it is argued, and on to an external object, the organism is engaged in life preservation. This refocusing of the death instinct to an external object comes about by the coupling of the life instinct with the death instinct. Hall (ibid., p. 101) describes this process:

> The death instinct, for example, is projected outward by the ego in the form of destruction, aggression, mastery, dominance, exploitation, and competition. This means that external objects are substituted for the original object-choice which is the person himself. As long as the energy of the death instincts can be deflected away from one's own person, danger is averted and the person does not feel anxious.

Aggression, then, can be viewed as intrinsic to human behaviour, and serves as a fundamental and essential means by which humans protect and enhance their existence. Aggression, from this Freudian perspective, is carried out in the name of self-preservation, and is inherent to humans.

By extension, then, it may be said that a Freudian perspective on conflict is based upon the interplay between the life and death instincts. As aggression may be the externalization of the death instinct, conflict more generally may be from a similar source.

Whereas Freud focused on the psychology of human action, others have focused more explicitly on the evolutionary and biologically competitive nature of human aggression and conflict. A notable proponent of 'aggression as a tool of survival' is Konrad Lorenz, author of *On Aggression*. The book, first published in 1963, expounds a theory outlining the purpose of aggression, not only in humans, but throughout the animal world. Like Freud, Lorenz argues that aggression serves a purpose in that it in some way assists the organism in its quest for survival. Rapoport (1986, p. 3) holds that at its most elemental 'aggressive behavior does confer a survival advantage on the species in which it is genetically imbedded'. Lorenz sees aggression in its most basic form as serving three primary functions: 'balanced distribution of animals of the same species over the available environment, selection of the strongest by rival fights, and defense of the young' (Lorenz, 1971, p. 40).

He argues for a special emphasis on the value of intra-species aggression, stating:

> I return to the theme of the survival value of the rival fight, with the statement that this only leads to useful selection where it breeds fighters fitted for combat with extra-specific enemies as well as for intra-specific duels. The most important function of rival fighting is the selection of an aggressive family defender, and this presupposes a further function of intra-specific aggression: brood defense. (ibid., p. 39)

He makes his argument using a host of examples from throughout the animal world, including *Homo sapiens*.

The process of aggression is stimulated by instinct, which Lorenz notes as a much misunderstood mechanism. For Lorenz, instinct does not respond easily to manipulation, if at all. Like Freud, Lorenz sees instinct as something over which people have no control; it simply happens. Aggression, then, is quite dangerous, in that nothing hinders its expression. Furthermore, instinct need not be expressed through external stimulus; the body itself can produce the stimulus needed to create the reaction. Thus aggression becomes a dangerous instinct because its expression appears beyond any simple predictive device.

Using a Lorenzian model, then, all human social action is targeted towards distribution of the population, selection of the strongest, and defence of the young. The human aggressive impulse also gets translated into social activities, such as warfare. As Lorenz (1971, p. 275) notes, 'we must face the fact that militant enthusiasm has evolved from the hackle-raising and chin-protruding communal defense instinct of our prehuman ancestors'. For Lorenz, then, warfare is as natural as any other form of human aggression. Perhaps the only difference between the aggression of, for example, the rat and humans is that humans have developed an extensive and elaborate mechanism for pursuing that aggression.

Yet if human aggression focuses on population distribution, selection of fitness and defence of the young, then it is difficult to explain many acts of 'altruism', such as empowerment of the physically and mentally handicapped. From a Lorenzian perspective such action flies in the face of the purpose of intraspecies aggression.

Following the path of Lorenz, Robert Ardrey, in *The Territorial Imperative*, examined the role of territory in the onset of aggression. His objective was to examine the role of territory in humans. He wrote:

> The concept of territory as a genetically determined form of behavior in many species is today accepted beyond question in the biological sciences. But so recently have our observations been made and our conclusions formed that we have yet to explore the implications of territory in our estimate of man. (Ardrey, 1967, p. 14)

For Ardrey, territory represents a tremendous influence over human action, and even influences the ways in which humans form social groups. Ardrey (ibid., p. 15) asks, 'How could it be that such a number of peoples in such varying environments so remote from each other should all form similar social groups based on what would seem to be a human invention, the ownership of land?' Of course, Ardrey's observation of the ubiquitous nature of land ownership would be compelling if it were true, but evidence shows that there is no universal concept of land ownership. It would be more true to say that groups have a notion of physical place, without the connotation of ownership.

Relating territoriality to human behaviour, Ardrey (1967, p. 15) argues that:

> The principal cause of modern warfare arises from the failure of an intruding power correctly to estimate the defensive resources of a territorial defender. The enhancement of energy invariably engendered in the defending proprietor; the union of partners welded by the first sound of gunfire; the biological morality demanding individual sacrifice, even of life: all of the innate commands of the territorial imperative act to multiply the apparent resources of a defending nation.

Territory becomes the single most influential force in driving human action. Aggression, unlike in Lorenz's model, does not directly serve the species as such, but rather the group, as defined by territory. The drive to defend territory leads humans to increase their resources, multiply their activities and place themselves in mortal danger. Yet like Lorenz, Ardrey creates a picture of aggression in which humans have no control; they are enslaved by their own evolutionary history. In fact, Ardrey paints a grim picture for the future of humanity's ability to handle conflict:

> The human predicament contains two forces: On the one hand that balance of terror, the *pax atomica*, compels a general peace. ... In any event, war as we have known it has become both an impractical outlet for our innate psychological needs and an impractical external pressure enforcing our social amity. But on the other hand man's cultural achievements have long since pressed him beyond a point of possible return, and if he is to survive on his irreversible course of technological mastery, specialized skill, and consequent interdependence, then he becomes with every passing year, every passing day, more at the mercy of social amity and mutual co-operation.
>
> And so we must ask: Have our cultural achievements in peacetime, eliminating the reality of natural hazard, matched our cultural achievements in wartime, eliminating the reality of enemies, so that in final sum we must face that primate impossibility, exaggerated by human achievement, reduction to zero of effective amity? (ibid., p. 257)

Ardrey captures a central dilemma of handling conflict: how can one balance on the one hand the territorial imperative against the creation of a culture of cooperation? Can a culture of cooperation overcome millions of years of evolution? Ardrey's answer is not promising: overcoming evolution is not possible. Military historian John Keegan (1993) makes many of Ardrey's observations but concludes, however, that warfare is indeed dead.

Of course there is ample room to ask where culture begins and evolution ends. There can be little doubt that territory, either symbolic or real, is an important influence on any conflict behaviour. Whether, though, it represents such a strong, and genetically based, behaviour is quite another question. There may be another subtle distinction to be made. It may also be possible that there is a biological basis to physical territory and a different, for example cultural, basis to symbolic territory. Ardrey's thesis, while in many ways attractive, has yet to answer these and other questions.

What the work of Ardrey does provide, though, is some insight into the possible origins of nationalism and ethnicity. It could be argued that nations are the logical extensions of groupings of human beings, who perceive themselves as a group. In defining itself as a group, that collective then behaves aggressively to those who are not its members.

A final ethnographer examined is Frans de Waal, author of *Peacemaking among Primates*. Unlike Lorenz and Ardrey, de Waal focuses on the role of reconciliation between primates, and argues that peacemaking is the natural and logical adjunct to innate aggression. Picking up on the Lorenzian claim of an innate drive to aggression, de Waal suggests that such a slavish commitment to aggression would not yield a cohesive society. He believes, though, that the Lorenzian aggression is guided by a sense of in-group/out-group difference. He submits that safety measures have evolved in animals to temper aggressive drives. De Waal (1989, p. 11) adds:

> Even crocodiles, archaic animals with powerful jaws, may be seen walking around with a mouthful of trusting youngsters, who look out from between their mother's teeth like sightseers from a bus. The more complex the group life of animals becomes, the more remarkable the inhibitions that can be observed, not only towards kin but also toward unrelated members.

Employing classic deterrence reasoning, de Waal (ibid., p. 11) suggests that the quickest method of countering aggressive escalation is through 'soothing remarks or body contact'. Primates, including humans, de Waal argues, have developed an intricate system of behaviour to counter aggression. This behaviour, furthermore, is innate, and is expressed primarily within the context of one's own group.

Like Lorenz and Ardrey, de Waal also argues that not all aggression is necessarily negative. Aggression, he says, serves as a method of creating the sense of a group. Unlike many other theorists, de Waal is not suggesting that it is aggression against some outside group, but rather aggression within the group. Cohesion is created, for example, by the practice of hazing, where young military cadets in military academies undergo rituals, such as cleaning toilets with toothbrushes, or standing guard in the nude. These entail aggression on the part of group members towards members of their own group. Yet from the perspective of the group, the aggression may have been 'useful'. For de Waal peace comes, then, not out of some sense of equitable turning of swords into ploughshares, but rather through the acceptance of aggression, and of the reconciliation offered by other group members. In a sense, peace is the acceptance of inequality, the recognition that some are of a more equal status than others. To use de Waal's (1989) phrase, 'unification through subordination' may be the norm, though there is room for egalitarian resolution of conflict. It is just that egalitarian conflict resolution is not the norm.

What is encouraging about de Waal's work is that he looks more directly at humans when asking whether aggression is innate or not. Furthermore, he makes the sensible proposition that if aggression is ubiquitous and innate, then peacemaking must be too. Yet even with de Waal's reasonableness there are many questions left unanswered regarding the issue of the source of human aggression.

Keith Webb (1986) has outlined the common characteristics shared by inherency theories. These are:

- The fundamental disposition of individuals is towards power and dominance; violence is only an extreme but normal expression of this tendency.
- There are alternative channels for seeking power, of which collective political violence is merely one.
- The major problem is explaining why violence does not occur more often.
- The choice of violence is a question of tactical consideration.
- Tactical choices are influenced by cost–benefit calculations.
- Cultural factors play a relatively minor role, and will both inhibit and promote the use of violence.
- Factors such as the coercive balance of forces and facilitating conditions are of major importance.

The positive function of violence and aggression must also be added to the list, reflecting the work of theorists such as de Waal.

Contingent Theories

Counterpoised to the inherency arguments of the sources of human aggression are contingency theories. Contingency theories postulate that aggression is not innate, but its expression depends upon factors external to the person. As Webb (1986, p. 172) explains, 'Conflict may occur through a scarcity of and competition for resources, or through maldistribution of ample resources, but it may not be a necessary condition of human societies that these conditions pertain.'

The earliest 'modern' presentation of the contingency argument can be found in the writing of the French philosopher Jean Jacques Rousseau. Rousseau saw humanity as having moved from a state of nature to one of society, and social intercourse. In addition to humanity's 'desire for self-preservation, which Hobbes had found basic to man, Rousseau added compassion, the instinctive abhorrence felt at the sight of another living being, and especially another man, suffering pain and death' (Germino, 1972, p. 98). This compassion militates against the pure aggression and constant warfare found in Hobbes's works. Alone, humans are not innately aggressive or warlike. Ultimately, though, Rousseau notes humanity's creation of society, and thus comes the fall. It is not just any society that creates difficulty for people, but rather it is entry into the wrong sort of society. The goal, writes Rousseau, is

> To find a form of association which defends and protects with the entire common force the person and goods of each associate, and in which each uniting himself to all obeys only himself and remains as free as before – such is the fundamental problem of which the social contract gives the solution. (Rousseau, quoted in Germino, 1972)

The difficulty, of course, is that not all (or even many) forms of social association defend or protect the individual. Thus, it seems that society often hinders an individual from obtaining what is necessary to their happy and productive life. Rousseau encapsulates his perspective nicely when he writes, 'Man is born free, and everywhere he is in chains.'

The impact of Rousseau on later political theorists is notable. Perhaps the most important of his followers was the German philosopher Karl Marx. Marx's theory of class conflict was built upon a contingency argument. He argued that humans are separated from their true nature by the organization of work. Workers are controlled and dominated by economic factors beyond their direct control. This economic system, termed capitalism, is an arrangement whereby the producers of labour are alienated from the fruits of their labour. So, a person may make a chair, but it is not their chair; the chair is owned by somebody else, who secures the chair from the labourer. In so doing, the producer of the chair does not receive an equitable exchange and is thereby kept in bondage to the capitalist.

The class of people who belong to the capitalists are pitted against the labouring class, or those who are alienated from their products. This tension is expressed in terms of class conflict, and is the engine by which conflict itself ends. Evolution of communism takes hold, wherein, first, political communism arises, with the state still intact. The second stage is where the state is transcended, yet it is a condition in which the owners of private property still have influence. A final stage is entered into where there is 'a genuine resolution of the antagonism between man and nature and between man and man; it is the true resolution of the conflict between existence and essence' (Marx quoted in Germino, 1972). Like Rousseau, Marx felt that society and the development of society dramatically transformed humanity's condition. Whether conflict existed or not was dependent upon society, not the behaviour of individuals.

Some may argue that Marx's theories do not really fit well into the inherency/contingency split. Because of Marx's emphasis on history − that this is, for example, the historical epoch of the capitalists − it is difficult to know whether he is a contingency theorist or an inherency theorist. All human relations are conflictual, Marx argues, because of the historical (capitalist) epoch in which we live. The ironclad nature of such an argument suggests that there is something inherent in human behaviour. Yet the transition out of this historical epoch is in human hands, and not innate. Thus, for some Marx's theory rests on the precipice between inherency and contingency.

One of the most important issues that Marx brings to the fore is the role of economic and social organization and their collective impact on human behaviour. In the early part of the twentieth century John Maynard Keynes, the noted British economist, brought attention to the flaws of European economic organization following the end of World War I and into the Great Depression. Keynes was not in any sense a Marxist; he was a follower of the democratic liberal tradition. To Keynes, the main social problems that he encountered included unemployment, disease and hunger. These are the causes of human misery and humans can act in ways to prevent them. It is the duty of government, then, to use its powers to influence the economy by stimulating investment, through a variety of means.

Keynes did not see humanity as innately tied to economic deprivation. He wrote:

> But what counsel of hope can Revolution offer to sufferers from economic privation, which does not arise out of the injustices of distribution but is general? The only safeguard against Revolution ... is indeed the fact that, even to the minds of men who are desperate, Revolution offers no prospect of improvement whatever. (Keynes, 1920, p. 296)

The alternative to the inadequate revolution was, of course, an economic system which provided for an increase in the general welfare of the citizenry. Implied throughout, of course, is the concept that deprivation, poverty and hunger are causes of social conflict. This underscores many an economist's theories of human behaviour. Where Marx saw the state as, ultimately, working against the interests of humanity, Keynes saw it as perhaps the only alternative to social decay and violence. Keynes was neither the first nor the last to suggest that the state could resolve the ills which frustrated humanity's existence.

Implicit in many contingency theories is the argument that when humans are faced with a force that frustrates their normal behaviour, they become aggressive. It was not until 1939 that this was formally articulated by several Yale University academics. Primary among them were John Dollard, Neal Miller and Leonard Doob, who collaborated to write *Frustration and Aggression*. They put their case most succinctly:

> This study takes as its point of departure the assumption that *aggression is always a consequence of frustration* [emphasis original]. More specifically the proposition is that the occurrence of aggressive behavior always presupposes the existence of frustration and, contrariwise, that the existence of frustration always leads to some form of aggression. (Dolland *et al.*, 1964, p. 1)

This seemingly rigid link between frustration and aggression, however, was in need of modification. One can easily see that not all frustration leads to aggression — at least certainly not in any immediate sense. Most people in a traffic jam do not jump out and start assaulting those around them, though many may feel the impulse. Clearly, the relationship between frustration and aggression is more complex. It is also clear that aggression is not the only response to frustration. For example, it has been argued that frustration can lead to individuals becoming helpless. In the face of ongoing frustration, parties may, instead of becoming aggressive, acquiesce and simply surrender as a coping mechanism. Martin Seligman (1975) described coping helplessness as learned helplessness. It is equally unclear what is meant by frustration and what causes frustration. Is frustration always from an external source? Is a frustrating event an objective phenomenon, or subjective, or both? Equally difficult is aggression. Is aggression always a physical act? Is there such a thing as symbolic aggression? Is there such thing as internalized aggression, and if so, how do we know? Can frustration be stored up, to result in aggression at a later date? While Dollard *et al.* seek to address many of these questions, they do so in a sometimes less than convincing manner, so that these questions represent the many difficulties that impact upon the frustration–aggression hypothesis.

It is interesting to note that Dollard *et al.* did not limit themselves to the psychology of the individual, but also branched out into the world at large. One topic, for example, about which they wrote was racism. They explain:

> the existence of a social prejudice against a group of people is evidence, first, that those who have the prejudice have been frustrated and, secondly, that they are expressing their aggression or part of it in fairly uniform fashion. Race prejudice, then, can be explained with the help of the present hypothesis. (Dollard *et al.*, 1969, p. 151)

Racism, then, exists when the frustrated target their frustration on a group. That group, using this argument, may or may not be the source of the frustration, they may simply be scapegoats. In Australia, for example, European racism against Aborigines would be founded upon frustration felt among the European population, and result in aggression against the Aborigines. Of course, the Aborigines would feel frustrated having received the aggression of the European population and would themselves behave aggressively. A similar situation is found in the USA, Germany and elsewhere where groups are divided along racial or ethnic lines.

The difficulty, though, with this hypothesis is that it may not explain racism very well at all. In the Australian example the racism seems to have existed from the very outset of the founding of the penal colony. There was not really the buildup of any long-standing relationship between the Europeans and Aborigines before violence erupted. Instead, the violence seemed to occur almost instantaneously. Was the European reaction, then, displaced aggression, responding to frustration emanating from elsewhere? How will we know?

Placement of the frustration–aggression hypothesis in the contingency theory camp rests upon the observation that if there were no frustration, then there would be no aggression. By extension we may also say that if there were no frustration, then there would be no conflict. So, the expression of conflict seems to be dependent upon some factor outside the human organism.

Following on the work of Dollard *et al.* is that of B.F. Skinner. Skinner held that most behaviour was the result of learning, and that through operant conditioning organisms developed predictable patterns of behaviour. Skinner shifted the traditional focus from one of classical conditioning, most commonly associated with the Russian researcher Pavlov. Classical conditioning, for example, occurs when a dog is fed and every time the dog is fed a bell is rung. After several repetitions, the dog associates the ringing of the bell with food. So, the food and the bell become virtually synonymous, to the point that when the bell is rung and no food is given, the dog behaves as if food had been presented and salivates.

Operant conditioning works in a different way. It is based, essentially, on reinforcement. That is, a given behaviour is rewarded, and as the rewards accumulate, the behaviour becomes 'learned'. An example will suffice. A rat is placed in a box, into which the researcher randomly delivers food pellets through a special door. First, the rat learns that pellets come from this door. Next, the researcher stops delivering pellets of food, and the rat becomes hungry. As it searches the door for food it steps on a treadle, which releases a pellet of food. The rat eats the food. Next, the rat begins to search again, and once again steps on the treadle. After several repetitions, the rat learns that the treadle releases the food. Humans, much like rats in this respect according to Skinner, learn much of their behaviour in this fashion. They learn not only behaviour in general, but aggressive and conflictual behaviour specifically.

One of the best examples of the power of social learning came from work by Stanley Milgram. Milgram's work amply demonstrated the role of learning in social interaction. The now famous experiment that Milgram ran consisted of subjects who themselves thought that they were assisting in another experiment — when in fact they themselves were the experiment.

> Subjects were led to believe that they were participating in an investigation into the effects of punishment in learning situations. The role of the 'teacher' was assigned to a subject, and the role of the 'learner' to a person who, although posing as another subject, was actually a confederate of the experimenter. Learning consisted in associating nonsense syllables. (Rapoport, 1986, p. 5)

The 'teacher' gave electrical shocks to the 'subject' (i.e. experimenter's confederate) in each instance that the 'subject' made a mistake. As the 'subject's' mistakes continued, the intensity of the fictional shocks increased. With the increase in shock severity came the equivalent increase in apparent distress of the confederate. In the end, the 'teacher' was administering shocks that would have been, if real, injurious. While not every 'teacher' gave the injurious shocks, most did not quit the experiment, but continued even in the face of apparent injury and suffering.

The Milgram experiments provide clear illustrations of the lengths to which people will go in following 'the rules' and 'authority'. No one compelled the 'teachers' to permit the shocks to go on, they simply did what was asked of them. Clearly, this has implications concerning the sources of human behaviour. If we are conditioned to be aggressive, then we will follow the rules and be aggressive.

Following the work of Milgram is that of Albert Bandura, who argued that there are three primary sources of human aggression. Those sources are familial settings, subcultural context and symbolic modelling. Social learning takes place in the family, and from that environment we develop models of appropriate behaviour. Simply stated, Bandura's argument is that violent families produce violent offspring. By extension, then, it can be argued that conflictual families produce conflictual offspring.

A second source of aggression can be found in subcultures. Bandura (1973, p. 97) explains: 'The highest rates of aggressive behavior are found in environments where aggressive models abound and where aggressiveness is regarded as a highly valued attribute.' So, for example, in street gangs with a premium on violence, individual members of the gang would be expected to be violent. This is not too surprising, but Bandura (ibid., p. 98) asks not why people in violent environments should be violent, but 'why anyone residing in such an environment should adopt a markedly different style of life'. Why is it that a person raised in a violent environment may not be violent? Of course, one reason why people may not become violent is that many people may simply aspire not to be violent. Living in a violent environment does not make one an automaton, desiring only that which is readily available. This desire for things other than violence may lead parents to instil in children values and behaviours that are in and of themselves counter-violent. Bandura does suggest, though, that there is a strong capacity to instruct a group in the ways of violence. He makes his point in suggesting that the military is an excellent example of making otherwise relatively non-violent persons violent.

A final category of social learning comes from symbolic sources. Bandura argues that a major source for the transmission of violence is television. Television transmits pictures of violence, impressions of violence and even the symbolic culture of violence. We learn how to cope with 'reality' through television, and are susceptible to its messages. This is especially true among the young of society.

Television as a source of social learning, especially as a device for transmitting conflictual values, is an area that has been debated hotly over the years. There appears to be no easy answer to the question, primarily because it is so difficult to isolate television-watching behaviour from the rest of our social interactions.

Through the interaction of these three areas we are invested with the culture of violence and aggression, and given models of how to deal with conflict. Using Bandura's model it is possible to speak of a culture of conflict, an organization which is conflictual, or even a conflictual nation.

In sum, the contingency theory school holds that conflict and aggression are dependent upon factors outside the individual. In general, contingency theories hold:

- Individuals are basically pacific.
- Under special conditions the pacific impulses may be diverted.
- The major problem for conflict theory is to explain the frequency of violence.
- When special conditions arise, other human dispositions may be activated.
- Collective violence is affected rather than coolly calculated.
- The tendency to violence may be affected by cultural learning.
- Two further minor factors affecting the use of violence are coercive balance between forces and other factors facilitating the successful use of violence. (Webb, 1986)

It appears that the causes of aggression, and conflict, are very different according to the contingency school and the inherency school respectively.

Interactionist Approaches

A third school is the interactionist, which combines elements of the contingent and inherency schools. There really is no body of literature that rejects the premise that behaviour derives from *either* nature *or* nurture. Instead of debating this old and apparently unending debate it ought to be rejected outright. Wrangham and Peterson call the nature versus nurture debate Galton's Error, after Francis Galton, a cousin of Charles Darwin. Galton took the phrase 'nature versus nurture' from Shakespeare's *The Tempest*. Since then scholars have been engaged in trying to ascertain the relative contributions of the two. Wrangham and Peterson (1996) reject Galton's Error, arguing that it is a false choice. The best course is to cast off the reductionist impulse and instead focus on how both genetics and social interactions commingle to create human behaviour. Both the inherency and the contingency school suffer from difficulties that make exclusive reliance upon their assumptions questionable. The inherency school ignores social grouping, and when it does focus on such groupings, inherency theorists simply say society is what it is, and results from genetics. The contingency theorists also suffer some significant difficulties, prime among which is the inability to deal with clear biological limitations on human behaviour. For example, if intelligence is a matter of genetics, and has an influence over conflict behaviour, then how does the contingency school cope?

The interactionist approach is best illustrated by examining height. A tall person becomes tall, relative to others, through two influences. One influence is genetics: a person is tall in part because of his or her genetic constitution. The tall person, though, is also tall because of social factors, such as the availability of high-protein foodstuffs. Citizens of Japan are now increasing in average height, owing to a change in diet. It was not that the Japanese are genetically short, but rather that their diet inhibited the full expression of their genes for height. So, the height of the Japanese (and everybody else for that matter) is governed by the interplay between genetic make-up and social environment.

Burton has argued that needs satisfaction is essential to society. In this sense, his work reflects that of many of the inherency theorists. Human beings are motivated by a series of drives, or needs, which compel them to act. As Burton (1990, p. 36) explains, 'From the perspective of conflict studies, the important observation is that these needs will be pursued by all means available. In ontological terms the individual is conditioned by biology, or by a primordial influence, to pursue them.' Needs, however, do not exist in the biological world alone, but rather in a social milieu. Needs satisfaction behaviour is expressed socially, and so the social setting influences the degree to which they may be satisfied. In this sense, then, Burton's work also draws on contingency theory, in that the satisfaction of needs is dependent upon the social context.

An example of the interaction between inherency and contingency in the satisfaction of needs is found in an impoverished ethnic group. Burton would argue that this group has, among other needs, a need for security. This need will be pursued doggedly. The satisfaction of this need may come either collectively or individually. Whether it is satisfied depends upon not only the behaviour of the individual, but also what is available in society. As Burton argues, though, basic human needs are not scarce; there is no limit to security. Yet there may be social limits, in terms of acceptability. While theoretically a person may undertake any behaviour in order to satisfy a need, they may feel constrained by what is regarded as 'acceptable' social behaviour. Those who seek to satisfy needs by any means necessary are often labelled deviant. Those who fail to satisfy their needs and suffer accordingly also can be deviant, but instead can be labelled maladjusted, or even neurotic.

In the above example, people behave in many ways in order to satisfy their needs. Some will follow a conservative path, strictly adhering to their interpretation of 'civil' behaviour. Others, though, will seek other means, some labelled eccentric and others labelled 'anti-social'. Eccentric behaviours might be extreme forms of religiosity; others might be forms of nationalism. More 'extreme' behaviours, though, might be termed 'revolutionary' as individuals seek to secure their security needs. In many dispossessed groups there have been messianic movements, extreme forms of nationalism, and strict conservatism. All these behaviours can be understood through the need for security; that is, the need to make oneself secure.

The primary criticism to be levelled against the interactionist school is that it does not reduce behaviour to a simple cause. In this sense, it is perhaps not as satisfying as the inherency or contingency arguments. Some may see a rejection of the nature versus nurture question as surrender − a sort of intellectual throwing up of the hands. It would be unreasonable, though, to accept such criticism. The nature versus nurture argument is reminiscent of the alchemists' search for a way of converting iron into gold. Try as they might, they could not do it. It is likely that behaviour can never be reduced to a single cause.

In sum, the interactionist school holds the following:

- Individuals are often pacific, but violence as such is not aberrant.
- Conflict is one, but not the only response, to unmet needs.
- Human behaviour varies enormously, with impulses that are often not clear.
- Collective violence may be either reactionary or coolly calculated.
- The tendency to violence may be affected by cultural learning, tempered by inherent impulses.

The major problem for the interactionists is to explain how genetic and social forces interact.

One may feel that some of the indeterminate nature of the interactionist school is unsatisfying. After all, how can one say that the impulses of human behaviour vary enormously? One might expect or demand an answer. The simple reply to that is – why does there have to be an answer? Can there be many answers?

Conclusion: Where Assumptions Take Us

The manner in which one defines conflict, as well as the manner in which one uses theory, can lead to the asking of all sorts of questions that may not have been clear earlier. Equally, the manner in which one defines conflict and uses theory may cause all sorts of questions not to be asked. Essentially, both the definition of conflict and the use of conflict theory act as intellectual guides or maps for future activities. In the above attempts to define conflict it was clear just how diverse definitions can be, and just how difficult it can be to define what appears on the surface to be such an obvious concept. Equally, in trying to understand the sources of human behaviour it is apparent that there are many questions still in need of answering if one is going to comprehend the drives, impulses, constraints and influences which come to bear on human behaviour. How the sources of human behaviour are addressed has significant impact upon the specific theories of human behaviour that are formed. In the next chapter some specific theories of conflict are considered.

References

Ardrey, Robert (1967) *The Territorial Imperative*. London: Fontana Library.

Bandura, Albert (1973) *Aggression: A Social Learning Theory*. Englewood Cliffs, NJ: Prentice-Hall.

Baron, Robert, Norbert Kerr and Norman Miller (1992) *Group Process. Group Decision. Group Action*. Milton Keynes: Open University Press.

Bercovitch, Jacob (1984) *Social Conflict and Third Parties*. Boulder, CO: Westview Press.

Burton, John (1987) *Resolving Deep-rooted Conflict*. Lanham, MD: University Press of America.

Burton, John (1990) *Conflict: Resolution and Prevention*. New York: St Martin's Press.

Burton, John and Frank Dukes (1990) *Conflict: Practices in Management. Settlement and Resolution*. New York: St Martin's Press.

Coser, Lewis A. (1957) 'Social Conflict and the Theory of Social Change', *British Journal of Sociology* 8(3), 197–207.

de Waal, Frans (1989) *Peacemaking among Primates*. Cambridge, MA: Harvard University Press.

Deutsch, Morton (1973) *The Resolution of Conflict*. New Haven, CT: Yale University Press.

Dollard, John, Neal E. Miller, Leonard W. Doob, O.H. Mowrer and Robert R. Sears (1964) *Frustration and Aggression*. New Haven, CT: Yale University Press.

Folger, Joseph, Marshall Scott Poole and Randall K. Stutman (1993) *Working through Conflict*. New York: HarperCollins.

Freud, Sigmund (1990) 'Why War?: A Reply to a Letter from Einstein', in Paul Smoker, Ruth Davies and Barbara Munske (eds), *A Reader in Peace Studies*. Oxford: Pergamon Press.

Galtung, Johan (1990) 'Violence and Peace', in Paul Smoker, Ruth Davies and Barbara Munske (eds), *A Reader in Peace Studies*. Oxford: Pergamon Press.

Germino, Dante (1972) *Machiavelli to Marx*. Chicago: University of Chicago Press.

Hall, Calvin S. (1954) *A Primer of Freudian Psychology*. New York: Mentor Books.

Hobbes, Thomas (1974) *Leviathan*. Glasgow: Collins/Fontana.

Keegan, John (1993) *A History of Warfare*. New York: Alfred A. Knopf.

Keynes, John Maynard (1920) *The Economic Consequences of the Peace*. New York: Harcourt, Brace and Howe.

Kriesberg, Louis (1982) 'Social Conflict Theories and Conflict Resolution', *Peace and Change* 8(2/3), 3–17.

Lewin, Kurt (1997) *Resolving Social Conflicts and Field Theory in Social Science*. Washington, DC: American Psychological Association.

Lorenz, Konrad (1971) *On Aggression*. New York: Bantam Books.

Rapoport, Anatol (1960) *Games, Fights and Debates*. Ann Arbor, MI: University of Michigan Press.

Rapoport, Anatol (1986) 'Aggression', in Linus Pauling (ed.), *World Encyclopedia of Peace*, vol. 1. Oxford: Pergamon Press.

Schelling, Thomas (1980) *The Strategy of Conflict*. Cambridge, MA: Harvard University Press.

Seligman, Martin (1975) *Learned Helplessness*. San Francisco: W.H. Freeman and Co.

Simmel, Georg (1955) *Conflict*. New York: The Free Press.

Thorson, Stuart J. (1989) *Intractable Conflicts and Their Transformation*. Syracuse, NY: Syracuse University Press.

Tillett, Greg (1991) *Resolving Conflict*. Sydney: Sydney University Press.

Waltz, Kenneth Neal (1959) *Man, the State, and War*. New York: Columbia University Press.

Webb, Keith (1986) 'Conflict: Inherent and Contingent Theories', in Linus Pauling (ed.), *World Encyclopedia of Peace*, vol. 1. Oxford: Pergamon Press.

Wrangham, Richard and Dale Peterson (1996) *Demonic Males*. New York: Houghton Mifflin.

4
THEORIES AND THEORISTS IN CONFLICT RESOLUTION

In the preceding chapter the origins of human aggression and conflictual behaviour were examined. It was pointed out that human behaviour may be inherent — that is, determined by human biological structure — or it may be contingent — that is, growing from human social relationships. A third possibility is that it may be a mixture of the two, growing from both inherent human qualities and social conditions. Keeping the subject of the origins of human behaviour in mind, conflict resolution theory itself is now considered.

Much has been written on the theoretical basis of conflict and its resolution. Few authors make explicit connections between the theory of conflict and its resolution. It is the explicit link between theory and practice that now concerns students and scholars of conflict resolution. Burton has led the way in making the connection explicit, though there have been many others who have theorized on conflict and its resolution. In this chapter the major theorists of conflict resolution are examined. Few of those discussed in this chapter, however, have provided a unified theory of conflict which also specifically seeks to address the connection between theory and practice. Yet it is important to understand the intellectual antecedents that inform conflict resolution today.

Theory in Everyday Life

Many view theory as being the dry end of academic study. Often people will hunger for the action, believing theory to be the realm of people more interested in talking than acting. While there may be a kernel of truth to this idea, it is nonetheless sadly mistaken. Without theory, conflict resolution could not advance one step.

It has been noted that all people operate under two different types of theory. Argyris *et al.* (1990) distinguished between theories-in-use and espoused theories. Theories-in-use are those theories which we use day to day, and they are best reflected in our action. For example, in raising children an in-use theory might be best characterized by deterrence. Statements such as 'if you don't stop, you will be punished' reflect a deterrence approach to childrearing. Often theories-in-use are not articulated, and if you were to ask people what their theories of action were they could not tell you. Espoused theories, however, are those we can state. 'Children ought to be given an opportunity to describe the reasons for their actions' would be a theoretical statement of how children ought to be reared. Note that it may often vary from the reality of action. All conflict behaviour can be described in these two ways. It is the job of conflict resolution to sort through these two types of theory and discover what theories actually inform conflict behaviour and its resolution.

An even more fundamental task of theory, though, is to act as a road map for research and the asking of questions. Let me illustrate. If you wish to get from one end of town to another you must have a theory of how you are to do so. You could randomly act until you got to where you wished to be, but it would be a largely fruitless task, with no level of surety that you would ever get there. A theory is a tentative explanation of how you might get from point A to point B. This tentative explanation serves as a guide to action; it steers the actor towards some objective. In conflict resolution this is vital. Theory steers the would-be resolver towards some behaviours and away from others. Furthermore, theory also provides a feedback mechanism, so that if theory steers in an incorrect direction, the resolver can change action towards what might be a more fruitful course. Of course, this all presumes that the theorist knows what it is that he or she wishes to do, and has some sense of the lengths he or she wishes to travel in order to attain some end.

Thus the discussion of the development of theory in conflict resolution is vital in the understanding of the development of the field, and in ascertaining how and whether conflicts can be resolved.

Theorists

Since the mid-nineteenth century there have been a variety of theorists concerned with conflict, of whom Karl Marx was perhaps the most noteworthy. Marx's concern with class conflict, seated as it was in the grander context of political change, gave way in the twentieth century to a more focused study of conflict itself. Attention is given here to the work of a select few of the major theorists of conflict and its resolution. The intention here is not to mention every theorist who ever addressed the issue of conflict, but rather to examine briefly those who have had a major impact on the study of conflict resolution. Each in their own way has contributed to the field. Examining some of the more prominent theorists will make it clear that there remain questions in need of attention.

Simmel

A useful place to begin in examining the theorists of conflict and conflict resolution is with Georg Simmel. Simmel sought to study the role of the individual in small groups, as well as the role of small groups in a larger social context. Most notable of his works on conflict was his extended essay *Conflict* (1955). Simmel argues that conflict has an integrative nature, bringing together disparate and contending influences. Thus conflict in Simmel's terms integrates disparate members of a group into the group. That is, conflict socializes members into the group, bringing members together by integrating them into the group through the social force of conflict. In this way, then, conflict is a socialization process, reducing the tension existing between group members. Underlying all conflicts are contending dual forces. For instance, Simmel argues that there exists an innate human drive or need for sympathy. Juxtaposed against sympathy, however, is hostility. Simmel argues that humans have a need both of sympathy and of hostility. He (1955, p. 15) writes of this duality:

> Just as the universe needs 'love and hate,' that is, attractive and repulsive forces, in order to have any form at all, so society, too, in order to attain a determinate shape, needs some quantitative ratio of harmony and disharmony, of association and competition, of favourable and unfavourable tendencies.

Simmel argues that conflicts may end in one of three ways. They may end by victory of one party over another; through compromise;

or through conciliation. Not all conflicts, though, can be ended by one of these three methods. Some, usually those characterized by high levels of feeling, cannot be ended by compromise. Different still from compromise and victory is conciliation. Conciliation refers to the subjective state of mind, wherein the objective sources of conflict (e.g. resource distribution) may still apply, but the subjective beliefs may be such that the conflict ends. For example, a conflict between siblings serves the purpose of creating a synthesis within the family between their two contending forces. The siblings experience a clash between themselves, and from this grows a unity between actors. Thus both siblings become socialized into the context of the family group. They learn, presumably, a set of behaviours which, while not necessarily eradicating the clash between them, nonetheless constrain and limit the way in which they express their clash. The conflict between siblings may come to an end by way of one sibling winning over the other. The older sibling may use his greater strength in order to end a conflict with the younger sibling. Or the siblings may compromise over such things as resources, leaving aside any compromise over strong emotions, such as love or hate. Or, finally, they may employ conciliation to end the conflict, leaving the objective sources of conflict aside and focusing instead on the subjective sources.

Simmel's work is important in the study of conflict resolution because he clearly articulated a positive social function for conflict. Conflict, in Simmel's terms, was a source of social cohesion and creativity. While conflict may often, or even usually, have negative social consequences, it must also be recognized as having positive ones too. Yet Simmel did not explicitly discuss how to resolve conflict. Such recommendations are left for later writers.

Coser

Following the work of Georg Simmel, Lewis Coser, an American sociologist, articulated his own vision of social conflict. Like Simmel, Coser argued that conflict serves specific and useful social functions. He presented his thesis in his seminal work, *The Functions of Social Conflict*, first published in 1956, in which he argued that conflict serves a variety of useful purposes. Coser (1968, pp. 47–8) wrote:

> Conflict is not always dysfunctional for the relationship within which it occurs; often conflict is necessary to maintain such a relationship. Without ways to vent hostility toward each other, and to express dissent, group members might feel completely crushed and might react

by withdrawal. By setting free pent-up feelings of hostility, conflicts serve to maintain a relationship.

He thus saw conflict as serving a vital social function, serving to maintain established social relationships, which are deemed in some sense to be important to the functioning of society. Furthermore, he argued (ibid., p. 48) that institutions are created which 'drain off hostile and aggressive sentiments'. Clearly, though, some institutions are better at draining off hostility than others. Some institutions may be dysfunctional in how they administer hostility and aggression.

Coser also argued that conflict does more than drain hostilities, noting that:

> Conflict not only generates new norms, new institutions … it may be said to be stimulating directly in the economic and technological realm. Economic historians often have pointed out that much technological improvement has resulted from the conflict activity of trade unions through the raising of wage levels. (Coser, 1957, p. 198)

This presents an interesting difficulty for any who seek to resolve conflict. If Coser is correct, and conflict serves a socially useful purpose, then what conflicts should be resolved? Upon what basis will those seeking to resolve conflicts select the right conflicts to resolve?

Coser (1957, p. 198) observed that the resolution of conflict, for example in industry, 'may have unanticipated dysfunctional consequences'. That is to say, resolving industrial conflict may simply perpetuate inequities and improper work practices. There may be workplace conflicts that are better left unresolved, so that new and better methods of industry may be developed. Coser believes this may be overly reliant upon the unpredictable and uncontrollable vagaries of conflict, but it is nonetheless better, to paraphrase Kenneth Burke, than being 'unfitted by being fit in an unfit fitness' (ibid., p. 199). That is to say, a society that deals with its problems solely through the operation of ritual may be characterized by individuals who are well adapted to behaviours that in themselves are not particularly useful. This echoes Thorstein Veblen's concept of trained incapacity, wherein individuals become unable to resolve problems owing to their own training. Training leads individuals to do some things very well, but by the very fact of being trained, they do not do other things very well. Coser argues that conflict breaks people out of old and dysfunctional habits, and thus serves a positive social function.

The most important contribution that Coser made to the study of conflict was to focus the minds of researchers on the role that conflict plays in society — both the functional and dysfunctional roles. There may be considerable debate, however, over when conflict is functional and when it is dysfunctional. For instance, it may be functional for one group or segment of society, but it may equally be totally dysfunctional for another. While it might be seductive to ask whether in sum a given conflict is functional or dysfunctional, this presumes that such 'calculations' can be made, which may not be the case.

Neither Coser nor Simmel's work constituted a paradigm shift as such. Their insight into the positive aspects of social conflict did, however, provide an important shift in the emphasis in thinking, highlighting the possible positive characteristics of social conflict.

Lewin

Kurt Lewin, a German-born American academic, wrote extensively on the subject of conflict in the first half of the twentieth century. His contribution to the study of conflict is important for a variety of reasons. Most important of his contributions to the study of conflict was field theory. 'Field theory may be characterized as a method of analyzing causal relations and building scientific constructs' (Lippitt, 1968, p. 266). The basic elements of Lewin's field theory included (1) psychological explanations of behaviour, (2) consideration of the total situation, (3) systemic causation instead of historical, and (4) an approach characterized by dynamics. What is so significant about Lewin's work is that he attempted to integrate explanations of individual behaviour within a social context. For Lewin, the person did not exist apart from society, nor did society operate over and above the person, but rather they were integrated. Gordon Allport, writing in the introduction to Lewin (1997), argues that 'Lewin's outstanding contribution is his demonstration that the interdependence of the individual and the group can be studied in better balance if we employ certain new concepts.'

Key among Lewin's concepts is the idea of life space. Life space consists of two major components, the psychological environment and the person. By understanding the interaction between the person and the psychological environment, one can make predictions about a person's behaviour.

Another central point in Lewin's work was his emphasis on the role of needs satisfaction in the expression of conflict. Lewin (1997, p. 71) argues, 'Whether or not a particular event will lead to a conflict depends largely on the tension level or on the social atmosphere in the group.' Key sources of tension in conflict settings include needs satisfaction:

> A need in the state of hunger means not only that a particular region within the person is under tension but also that the person as a whole is on a higher tension level. This holds particularly for basic needs, such as sex or security. (ibid., p. 71)

Lewin was one of the earliest theorists of conflict to make explicit the connection between social humans and the satisfaction of their needs. Vital to the satisfaction of needs is that ability of the person to 'move'. Movement, in Lewin's sense, refers not to space, but rather to the capacity of an individual to have psychological space. Thus if individuals have little psychological space in which to move, then they will act to increase their freedom of movement by either changing their psychological space, or leaving the situation that constrains their movement.

Out of Lewin's work has grown a tripartite typology of conflict. The first type is approach–approach situations. In these situations individuals face two forces, both of which are attractive. The individual will be torn between selecting one or the other. As an individual approaches one of the two more closely, though, the attractive force of the other, the more distant, will decline.

A second type of conflict is avoidance–avoidance, where two forces are both undesirable. The individual may be forced to have to choose one of the two, or, in other situations, may be able to leave the situation, thus escaping the paired choice. So, a person might be faced with the unpleasant prospect of either taking a cut in pay for a more pleasant job, or keeping an unpleasant job. There may be no escaping this choice in times of high unemployment, whereas in times of high employment the person may be able to resolve the conflict by quitting the undesirable job.

The third type of conflict is termed approach–avoidance, where a person faces choices that comprise both positive and negative characteristics. So, for example, a person might face a situation where either they receive higher pay for their job, but work for a bad employer, or receive less money and work for a good employer. A variation of the approach–avoidance type is found in situations where a positive outcome can be obtained, but only by passing through negative events. So, for example, refugees seeking to escape warfare might have to experience increased danger by passing through an area of heavy combat.

Although this typology may not offer great explanatory power, it does provide a useful analytical and descriptive purpose. Lewin's work is, ultimately, of a very practical nature and meant to be applied to real situations. Reflecting this worldly orientation in Lewin's work, action research originated with him. Lewin held that leading practitioners and scholars could put their efforts to good social use. Action research links research, training and action leading to positive social change. Thus, for Lewin, there was a social responsibility that connected research and education. This clear bond between research, training and action has persisted in the study of conflict resolution.

Deutsch

Morton Deutsch is an American social psychologist who has made significant contributions to the study of conflict resolution. Central to his work has been the issue 'not [of] how to eliminate or prevent conflict but rather how to make it productive' (Deutsch, 1973, p. 17). Deutsch rightly notes that differentiating between constructive and destructive conflicts is easily done in extreme cases, yet these represent the overwhelming minority of cases.

One characteristic of destructive conflict is its expanding and escalating nature. Destructive conflicts, he argues, tend to be larger conflicts. Constructive conflicts are more constrained in their expression, and are smaller than the destructive type.

In conducting his research Deutsch (1991) has been guided by five assumptions.

1. Each participant in a social interaction responds to the other in terms of his perceptions and cognitions of the other; these may or may not correspond to the other's actualities.
2. Each participant in a social interaction, being cognizant of the other's capacity for awareness, is influenced by his own expectations concerning the other's actions as well as by his perceptions of the other's conduct.
3. Social interaction not only is initiated by motives but also generates new motives and alters old ones.
4. Social interaction takes place in a social environment – in a family, a group, a community, a nation, a civilization – that has developed

techniques, symbols, categories, rules and values that are relevant to human interactions.

5. Even though each participant in a social interaction, whether an individual or a group, is a complex unit composed of many interacting subsystems, it can act in a unified way towards some aspect of its environment.

Deutsch has been a forerunner in emphasizing the subjective nature of conflict. The subjectivist view holds that if somebody believes a conflict exists, then there is a conflict. Deutsch views conflict as essentially social despite the many influences that come to bear on an individual.

In Deutsch's view of conflict there are three factors which influence the probability of conflict's erupting. Those factors are contact and visibility of differences, perceived incompatibility, and perceived utility of conflict. Clearly, conflict will be heightened when parties are in contact with one another. It would be somewhat difficult for conflict to occur between parties if those parties had no contact between one another. The perception of visible differences will serve as visceral reminders of group membership. The anti-Semitism of Nazi Germany was fuelled, no doubt, by the requirement that Jews wear arm bands that clearly labelled them. Without that label it would have been more difficult for the government to perpetuate the existence of the conflict.

The perception of incompatibility clearly influences conflict behaviour as well. In perceiving that there is no ground for agreement between parties in conflict, there then (following this logic) becomes greater reason to engage in conflict. Believing that there can be no peace between believer and infidel makes conflict between them all the more likely. Even in situations where there may be no objective incompatibility, there still may be perceived incompatibility.

Finally, Deutsch identified the perceived utility of conflict as an important contributor to its expression. If cultural values, for example, hold conflict to be a reasonable and important way of dealing with perceived incompatibility of goals, then conflict behaviour will be used. Groups that have extensive histories in using conflict as a matter of policy will be more likely to engage in conflict in the future. Thus the utility of conflict will influence its use, as do perceived incompatibility, contact and visibility of difference.

Conflict resolution, Deutsch believes, is governed primarily by the development of skill. The more skilful the party, the more likely that the conflict will be resolved in an effective and efficient manner. 'Many destructive conflicts between nations, groups and individuals result from their lack of skills related to the procedures involved in constructive conflict resolution' (Deutsch, 1991, pp. 27–8). Thus he makes a clear link between the theory of conflict and its resolution. From Deutsch's perspective conflict resolution is facilitated by skills training.

In what skills, however, should parties be trained?

Key to resolving conflicts, in Deutsch's perspective, is the correction of perception, which is at the centre of all conflict. He argues, 'Impoverished communication, hostile attitudes, and over-sensitivity to differences – typical effects of competition – lead to distorted views that may intensify and perpetuate conflict; other distortions commonly occur in the course of interaction' (Deutsch, 1991, p. 43). The skills that parties need to overcome conflict, and which encourage the likelihood of resolution, are those that enhance accurate perceptions and stimulate communication between parties.

It is interesting to note that Deutsch differs markedly from Simmel, Coser and Lewin in a number of key ways. Simmel and Coser both held conflict to be a much more objective phenomenon, one that could be predicted by examining the exterior world. Deutsch views conflict as much more of an internal and subjective phenomenon which cannot be seen outside. The manifestations of the internal subjective state may be observed, but even then it is difficult to know exactly what is occurring. Neither Simmel nor Coser addressed the specifics of conflict resolution, though they both addressed the social role of conflict resolution. That is to say, Simmel and Coser addressed the impact of resolved conflict, but wrote little on how actually to resolve conflict. Lewin's main contribution in this sense was to link the individual and the social setting, thus focusing more on the subjective state of the being. Yet Lewin also did not make the explicit link between conflict and its resolution. He did identify action research as a possible avenue, but by itself it represented an insufficient base from which to practise conflict resolution. Deutsch may be credited with making the strongest link in conflict resolution theory between the understanding of conflict and its resolution.

Game Theorists

Game theory is the systematic study of problem-solving in cases where at least two interdependent parties are involved in seeking some outcome. It is used primarily by economists to study human problem-solving behaviour. Poundstone (1992) describes it as 'a rigorously mathematical study that evolves naturally from a reasonable way of looking at conflict'. It had its beginnings in the mid-twentieth century, and was considerably advanced by the guiding hand of mathematician John von Neumann and economist Oscar Morgenstern in their book *Theory of Games and Economic Behavior*. Anatol Rapoport, a co-founder of the *Journal of Conflict Resolution*, directly applied game theory to conflict resolution. Game theory is used to model the ways in which people will engage in conflict. Unlike Simmel and Coser, for example, who examine conflict as either functional or dysfunctional, or like Deutsch, who probes constructive and destructive conflict, game theory attempts to examine conflict as it is.

The study of human behaviour through the use of game theory is built around several key principles. First, it is assumed that people will make rational choices, from which they will estimate the probability of any given action and take only those actions that appear rational. Second, game theorists assume perfect knowledge: that is to say, when behaviour is modelled through game theory it is assumed that individuals know all there is to know and that neither party knows more than the other.

A key focal point of game theory is the examination of strategy, or the plans used in order to obtain a final objective. For example, a strategy may be described as cooperative, meaning that a party will agree with everything another party says or does. Other strategies may be competitive, but most are a mixture of both.

The most common encounter one has with game theory is in the game of chicken. Typically, two people driving cars racing towards the edge of a cliff illustrate the game. It focuses on flinching: that is, the first to flinch and steer away from the cliff's edge loses. As an illustration of conflict, chicken serves as useful illustration of brinkmanship. The Cuban missile crisis is a real-life example of chicken, where both the US and the USSR stood, metaphorically, toe to toe, waiting for the other to blink. When the USSR made the first public conciliatory move, it blinked and the game of chicken ended.

Another common representation of game theory is Prisoner's Dilemma. Imagine that two people are arrested for a crime, say theft. Police separate them for interrogation. Neither robber knows what the other will say, though they do have perfect knowledge of the range of possible outcomes. If one robber tells all, a reduced sentence will be given. If, on the other hand, the robber does not inform the police, he or she faces a chance of going to jail for ten years. In another cell, the other robber faces the same possible outcomes: tell all and get a small sentence, or say nothing and suffer the consequences. The difficulty is that if one tells all and the other does not, then the police will jail the 'squealer' and the other will go free. If they both squeal, then they both will get a light sentence. If neither says anything, then they both go to jail for the full sentence. So, the dilemma is that if Robber A, say, talks, A can escape with light punishment only if Robber B also talks, but A has no way of making B talk, and vice versa. Nor does either of them know what the other is doing. Thus the prisoners are in a dilemma.

Prisoner's Dilemma has been used to explain many conflict situations where the outcome of the conflict is dependent upon what each of the parties does, but neither of the parties knows with any certainty what the other will do. In this situation parties develop strategies to compensate for the lack of surety about the actions of the other party. The trouble is, though, that such strategies may lock parties into escalating conflict where none was necessary. Robert Axelrod, a political scientist, wished to study how parties may evolve a cooperative interdependent strategy. That is, using a Prisoner's Dilemma situation, he wished to discover how cooperation could evolve between parties when the game was characterized by mistrust. In *The Evolution of Cooperation* Axelrod reports on a number of experiments he conducted in an effort to discover how cooperation might evolve between parties. He ran computer programs in order to discover strategies that would engender cooperation. Of all the strategies provided, one of the simplest turned out to be the most effective. Anatol Rapoport's 'tit-for-tat' strategy was the winner. Tit-for-tat strategy is where one party mimics every move of the other party. Therefore, when one opponent is competitive, the other is competitive, and when the opponent is cooperative, the other is cooperative.

Game theory is a highly abstract method of modelling human conflict behaviour. Although it has the appeal of rigour, it fails in many significant ways. Among these is that it makes assumptions which are not particularly useful. Chief among those assumptions is rationality. People often do not make choices which are rational, and this seems especially so in conflict. Yet game theory, for all its abstractness, cannot be easily dismissed. It has provided a variety of useful insights into the process of conflict. One of the most important things that it has done is to highlight the role of perception in conflict. Parties may be more than willing to end a conflict, yet may not do so because they perceive the other party as engaging in conflict. Prisoner's Dilemma clearly illustrates this point. Game theory has also given to the study of conflict resolution some useful terminology. Win–win, for example, refers to events wherein both parties in a game obtain a positive payoff; this is also called a positive-sum game. A zero-sum conflict is a game in which one party wins and the other loses an equal amount. A negative-sum conflict is one in which both parties lose. These terms have found their way into the language of conflict resolution.

Of further importance is the growth of social psychology in the study of conflict resolution. The use of social psychology comes out of the useful employment of game theory models in experimental conflict settings. Since conflict is often hard to model (owing to the real-world constraints on creating conflict), social psychologists have done well to create methods which do a reasonable job of mimicking conflict. Many social psychologists who study conflict do so using game theory models. An excellent illustration of this approach to the study of conflict resolution is found in the experiments done by Dan Druckman, Ben Broome and Susan Korper (1988). Druckman *et al.* were interested in the effect of pre-negotiation workshops on the resolution of conflict. Students were put into a simulation where some engaged in sessions that revealed 'values' which might not have been identified in conventional negotiation. In these workshops participants did not discuss their bargaining positions as such, but learned about one another's values which informed those positions. It was revealed that participants in this experiment who knew of the others' values were more willing to be cooperative than those who did not know of the others' values. Yet many of the criticisms made of game theory itself can also be made against the social psychology school.

Game theory, because of its level of abstraction and assumptions, has not proven very useful in the day-to-day practice of conflict resolution, but it has proved to be an important intellectual tool for examining broader themes and ideas.

Conflict Transformation Theorists

A growing number of theorists are rejecting the notion of conflict resolution as such, and instead writing about conflict transformation. At its heart, the conflict transformation school asserts that conflicts are always in flux, and always being transformed into something else. A primary intellectual source that informs the conflict transformation school is the functionalist camp represented by Simmel and Coser. Väyrynen has argued that there is an implied value in conflict resolution, namely that all conflicts should be resolved. While this is probably an over-simplification on Väyrynen's part, it has informed the development of theory. In reaction, conflict transformation theorists have argued that many political conflicts are better off left being transformed, rather than being resolved.

Conflict transformation theory attempts to reflect that dynamic quality of actors' interactions with each other and with the environment as a whole. No conflict is left unchanged; rather all conflicts are in a constant state of change. The goal is to know how to transform them into something that is socially useful and non-destructive. Attempts at resolution of conflicts will change their dynamics, whether or not the resolution itself was successful (Väyrynen, 1991). Wallensteen notes that conflict resolution is concerned with purposefully seeking grounds of commonality between parties, whereas conflict transformation refers to a change in the relationships between parties. This change in relationship occurs through conflict resolution, but it also may occur should one party totally defeat another. In both cases, conflict transformation has occurred. Wallensteen (1991, p. 129) defines conflict transformation as 'a generalized learning from historical experience'.

According to Northrup (1989), the evolution of the school of conflict transformation centres on four assumptions found in conflict resolution:

1. Parties to conflict are rational.
2. Misperception constitutes a central cause of conflict.
3. Conflict resolution principles apply across social settings (i.e. labour, international, interpersonal).
4. High value is placed on peaceful resolution.

Conflict transformation is based upon a *rejection* of these assumptions. Northrup argues that parties to conflict may be rational, but are often rational in different cultural contexts — so that there is a culturally specific form of rationality. This leads directly to the notion of misperception, which 'does not seem powerful enough or a deep enough notion to deal with drastic differences in world views' (Northrup, 1989, p. 57). When considering long-festering and deeply entrenched conflicts, simple misperception fails as an explanatory tool.

Northrup also calls into question the notion that conflict processes are the same across all settings. She points out that conflicts may go through stages, demanding different treatments at different times.

Finally, she observes that peaceful solutions do not act like a flame to a moth; many parties would rather continue the fight than switch to peace.

Although it is arguable whether Northrup's recounting of what constitute the assumptions of conflict resolution in fact applies to many of or all those in conflict resolution, it is clear that the rejection of these assumptions has informed the development of conflict transformation. The view of conflict from this perspective is that conflict is a highly elastic, changeable process, and therefore any process which seeks to alter conflict must be equally dynamic and changeable. The focus of conflict transformation is to move an intractable conflict (or deep-rooted, if you prefer) to being one which is resolvable.

There is an ongoing attempt to link the theory of conflict transformation to the practice of transformation. A major contribution to date is the recognition that conflicts are dynamic and that they cannot be spoken about as if they were immobile. But there is more work to be done.

Problems in Theory

Each of the conflict theorists mentioned thus far has highlighted different characteristics and aspects of conflict. Some common themes run throughout, but differences also exist. Underlying all these theories have been assumptions about human action and behaviour. Also couched in each of these theoretical approaches have been assumptions about the value of conflict resolution. Lewin, for example, clearly thought that conflict resolution was an important social goal, thus he developed action research. Game theorists, however, do not make such an assumption. Thus Lewin's approach has within it a prescriptive aspect, whereas game theorists are largely descriptive. None of these theories, though, is seen to be a comprehensive account of conflict and conflict resolution. None attempts to generate a complete theoretical explanation of conflict and its resolution. One of the few theorists who have attempted to create a generic theory of conflict resolution is John Burton. Before we turn to his work, however, it is important to turn first to the issue of paradigms.

Paradigms

Much of the discussion of theory in conflict resolution is prefaced by a deliberation on paradigms. The term paradigm has become a much-used word in academic discourse. It refers to a set of assumptions about the way in which the world operates. Kuhn (1970) argued that the operation of normal science, when faced with the need to explain what becomes increasingly unexplainable, becomes rigid and defensive. Against the operation of 'normal science' there arises a revolution against the popular and mainstream paradigm. Once 'normal science' gives way, a paradigm shift occurs, wherein the old assumptions about the way that the world works are rejected and new assumptions put in their place. As Sandole (1993) describes, 'Different paradigms, different mappings of the "same thing," mean different "realities" – different descriptions and explanations of the "same thing", plus a different sense of problems appropriate to that "thing" and of methods relevant to solving them.' Thus two people use different paradigms to look at a candle: both might see the same object, but the meaning of that object will be different for each. Furthermore, the questions raised about that candle – its origins, the time it takes to burn, its purpose – all depend upon the paradigm that is employed.

Sandole (1993, pp. 3–4) underscores the importance of the concept of a paradigm:

> That there may be multiple, and indeed, even *competing conceptions/ reconstructions of 'reality'*, even (but clearly, not only) in the sciences, makes the concept of 'paradigms' particularly relevant to conflict and conflict resolution where parties are quite prepared to die and to kill to defend their *competing* worldviews.

Paradigms play a significant role in the study of conflict resolution. Parties to a conflict may have very different conceptions of reality, or paradigms, and recognizing those differences is vital for resolution.

The discussion of paradigms, however, has had far greater significance in conflict resolution. Burton and Sandole (1986, p. 338) argue that 'during the 1960s a shift of a fundamental character was beginning to take place in behavioural studies, including biology, that established a consensus. This shift made possible the establishment of an *adisciplinary* study of conflict analysis and resolution.' Included in this shift was the rejection of power as the primary unit of analysis in international relations theory. It has been argued that the model of human behaviour was one in which humans were viewed as innately aggressive. Institutions operated to impose control on an otherwise unruly world, filled with aggressive people. Yet it seems that no matter how much coercive power is used to

impose order and control, there are always people who will seek
(even to their own destruction) to ignore the use of power and do
what they wish to do. The fundamental question, then, becomes 'Why
does deterrence fail to deter?' What constitutes a sufficient level of
power to keep people behaving as they 'should'? Conflict resolution
was born out of this paradigm shift. As an answer to these questions
it was posited that conflict stems from unsatisfied needs, and that
humans will do whatever they can to satisfy their needs. Furthermore,
needs satisfaction occurs within a social context.

The touted paradigm shift in conflict resolution has not been
without its critics. Most notable are Avruch and Black, who argue
that there is nothing revolutionary in the purported paradigm shift of
conflict resolution. Specifically, they argue that placing needs at the
centre of explanation of human behaviour is a throwback to the late
nineteenth century. Avruch and Black (1987) echo the well-worn
path of many anthropologists and sociologists, such as Dorothy Lee,
who denied that there were such things as human needs. Disciplines
such as anthropology and sociology play a key role in questioning
the existence and efficacy of the conflict resolution paradigm.

Among the pivotal components of this shift is the development
of a perspective which rejected the intellectual divisions of the past.
One could not, it is suggested, see the world through the lenses of
only biology, or anthropology; something other was needed. These
disciplines grew out of a paradigm where power was the major
method for human 'control' and explained social and individual
intercourse. The disciplines also reflect the increasingly irrelevant
nature versus nurture debate. Biologists are unconcerned with
social forces, cultural anthropologists reject biological explanations
of behaviour, and so on. The current disciplinary approach to
human behaviour would have us believe, if anybody took it
seriously, that behaviour can be separated into biological,
psychological, cultural sources. People, however, cannot be so
neatly chopped apart.

In lieu of this intellectual mincing of human behaviour a more holistic approach is suggested. This perspective reflects a more holistic
and all-encompassing view of human behaviour. At its core, this
holistic perspective serves to identify and account for the totality of
human relationships, and the totality of sources of human behaviour,
in order to highlight the integrated nature of humanity. The challenge, of course, is to recognize that one may never know the
totality of human relationships, but the goal is to keep focused on
new discovery, and new integration into the whole. Thus the

understanding of the totality of human behaviour is an ever-evolving process, one that continually integrates new understanding.

The theoretical basis for conflict resolution is therefore built, in part, upon a rejection of many of the ways in which human behaviour has been explained in the past. This is reflected in the manner in which conflict resolution draws on such a breadth of intellectual traditions: no one tradition by itself is sufficient, though each may bring to bear some useful and important information. As the various theorists are discovered, one should consider what assumptions they employ. Few theorists of conflict make any explicit claims of a paradigm shift. Yet couched within their work may be elements that inform that shift.

Burton

John Burton, an Australian academic and one-time Permanent Secretary of the Australian Department of External Affairs, has written extensively on conflict resolution.

Burton considers that the study of conflict resolution is, at its heart, a study of human behaviour and relationships. It is insufficient to study only 'psychological man' or economic behaviour. Rather, Burton argues for a holistic approach, wherein the entirety of the human, person and social, is studied. He further believes that a paradigm shift has occurred, wherein deterrence and power no longer explain social control. Human behaviour is represented by a broad diversity of forces, many of which are influenced by socialization. That is, humans are socialized into types of behaviour, into adapting social norms, that in and of themselves do not satisfy their needs. Socialization upholds societal needs, but may not necessarily do anything for the individual. From this observation has grown the human needs approach. Burton sees satisfaction of human needs as being the primary source of human behaviour. Furthermore, the satisfaction of needs cannot be understood outside the social context. Therefore, the study of human behaviour requires at once the study of the total individual, but in the social context.

In conflict, it is argued, humans will make statements about what is at issue, and these statements will reflect their interests, not their more fundamental needs. When humans engage in conflict, represented by their issues, they will use power and coercion in an attempt to get those needs satisfied. Thus by imposing their power relationships on others, needs satisfaction can become not the source of conflict reduction, but the cause of conflict. It is a paradox of human behaviour that in attempting to satisfy our basic needs we create conflict.

Burton has argued that what is needed in resolving conflict is a method wherein the causes of conflict can be analytically understood, and a method wherein traditional power bargaining does not take place. This is often referred to as an analytical, problem-solving approach. Institutions often make conflict resolution difficult, because they protect and defend the current power bargaining status. Resolution of conflict grows directly from an understanding of human social relationships. It rejects the basic premise that coercion and power are the basis upon which conflicts are resolved.

'Needs' refers to basic human requirements for the continuation and propagation of life. Much of the work on human needs in conflict resolution is based upon the works of Maslow, Sites and Burton. The existence of human needs is also, perhaps, the most problematic area of conflict resolution.

Maslow is credited with developing a theory of human needs, according to which the satisfaction of needs leads to healthier and more capable human beings. He differentiated between physiological needs (such as food), safety needs (need for structure, order or law), belongingness and love needs (friendship, inclusion), esteem needs (high evaluation of self), the need for self-actualization (being all that one can be). Maslow related the satisfaction of these needs to conflict. He noted that one must

> make the distinction between a deprivation that is unimportant to the organism (easily substituted for, with few serious after effects) and, on the other hand, a deprivation that is at the same time a threat to the personality, that is, to the life goals of the individual, to his defensive system, to his self-esteem, to his self-actualization, i.e. to his basic needs. (Maslow, 1987, pp. 105–6)

Important needs of which individuals are deprived, then, lead those individuals to seek to satisfy their needs. The manner in which they seek to satisfy their needs is open to question: they may seek any means necessary, even those that may put them or others in danger of physical harm.

Adding to the extensive literature on Maslow's theory of needs, Paul Sites (1973, p. 7), in his book *Control: The Basis of Social Order*, argued that 'basic needs do exist and that they are more universal, and thus less specifically cultural, than some behavioural scientists would have us believe'. Sites holds that basic human needs differ from those posited by Maslow. He put forward several, among them the need for identity, the need for stimulation, the need for control. The need for control, to Sites, is the strongest of all needs. By controlling one's environment one can also control the satisfaction of the host of other needs.

In placing needs at such a deep, universal level, Sites pitted culture against more generically human behaviour. This has had ramifications, as will be seen.

Burton has picked up Sites's thesis and has since argued:

> We are asserting that if there were to be discovered a definite set of human needs on the basis of which societies could be harmonious, major methodological problems in behavioural sciences and in policy-making would be avoided. If there were agreement as to human needs then there would be a logical starting point of behavioural analysis, for there would be a scientific basis for determining goals. (Burton, 1979, p. 63)

The Burtonian thesis, then, is that there are a set of *knowable basic human needs*, which serve as a guide to the understanding of human behaviour, and also act to steer policymakers in making decisions which will not lead to conflictual relationships. These needs are:

- consistency in response
- stimulation
- security
- recognition
- distributive justice
- appearance of rationality
- meaning
- control
- role defence (defence of roles that permits the satisfaction of needs).

A traditional criticism of all needs approaches is that it is always difficult to know just how many needs there are. In Burton's list, why are there only nine? Exactly how do we know that these are, in fact, needs and not something else? How do we disentangle cultural practices from needs? These points have been raised against virtually all needs schemes.

For Burton, conflict stems from unsatisfied human needs. Needs go unsatisfied because institutions have been designed from the context of power, and from the perspective of needs satisfaction. A primary difficulty in satisfying needs rests in the use of power. Power, or the use of coercive measures, acts as the method used by some to satisfy their needs. In using power to satisfy needs, one behaves in such a way as to satisfy one's own needs, while removing needs satisfaction from others. From a power perspective, if an institution satisfies needs, it does so only by accident. As Burton (1993) argues, people will not easily accept institutional arrangements that deny the satisfaction of their human needs. To Burton, the only way society can manage to prevent conflict is to ensure the satisfaction of everyone's basic human needs.

The way in which human needs can help resolve conflict is demonstrated in the following example. In his university lectures Burton has often used the example of the Falklands/Malvinas conflict between the UK and Argentina. While the ostensible conflict – that is, the issue conflict – was between the two states over the issue of sovereignty, Burton argues that it was much subtler. The conflict, according to Burton, was more over the needs of identity and recognition. The UK sought to maintain its identity of strength and further wished the Falkland Islanders to keep the identity of British subjects. By contrast, the Argentinians wished the islands to fly the flag of Argentina, though they had little interest in actually administering them. Thus a needs approach may be the only one capable of identifying the 'real' issues.

While Burton's Falklands/Malvinas example is interesting, it seems that these talks had little impact on later negotiations between the UK and Argentina. Furthermore, there is no reason to believe that every conflict will so easily and neatly raise basic human needs which are so easily and conveniently addressed. As Pruitt and Carnevale (1993, p. 40) note, 'Underlying concerns are sometimes no more amenable to settlement than surface issues.'

Burton has been roundly criticized, however, in his view of basic human needs, and in his methods of resolving conflict. Avruch and Black (1987), both cultural anthropologists, have taken Burton to task over his development of a generic theory of conflict resolution, and bring to bear the same criticisms concerning the issue of needs that have been raised against needs theorists many times in the past. What Avruch and Black suggest with particular reference to Burton is that the concept of role defence is fraught with particular difficulty. (Role defence refers to the need for defending the roles taken which satisfy other needs. So, if one's role is that of captain of a sailing ship, and one's needs are met by being in command of that ship, then one will seek to defend that role. Burton argues that the most difficult need to work with is role defence; it is also the one most subject to a win–lose power approach, in that people will often behave in dogged defence of their role. It is also the one key to all other needs because role defines the ability to satisfy other needs.) Avruch and Black also criticize Burton's work for failing to provide a method by which needs can be tested for their existence, or whether needs satisfaction does indeed lead to a reduction in conflict.

Burton's work on the origins of human social conflict is filled with difficulties, as his critics clearly illustrate, yet there is little doubt that it stands as some of the most influential and creative conflict resolution scholarship to date.

Criticisms notwithstanding, it is clear that most theorists believe that in order to successfully address conflict, it is not enough to focus only on the obvious, ostensible issues; one must look more deeply at the behaviour of parties in conflict. The Burtonian thesis, however, is unique in positing a set of needs which cut across all conflicts, in all times and all places.

A Troubled Paradigm Shift

It would be wrong to believe that conflict resolution has been talked about only within the context of a paradigm shift. This is not so. There are many authors who have addressed themselves to conflict resolution without mentioning the word paradigm, including some of the authors mentioned in this chapter. For example, Deutsch has long taken a social-psychological perspective to conflict resolution. He sees the basis of conflict as self-fulfilling prophecy, misperception and over-commitment. Thus, from this perspective, dealing with conflict is really a matter of clarifying perceptions, of both the self and the other, and taking 'rational' and realistic account of the likelihood of behaviour. There are, though, significant problems with this approach to conflict resolution. Some difficulties in Deutsch's theories are briefly outlined to illustrate the way in which the paradigm shift argument can rescue the theorist from troubled waters.

A significant difficulty in resolving conflict is misperception, according to Deutsch. What exactly is meant by 'misperception'? Use of the word suggests that there is an implied objective reality, over which people could agree, if only they perceived things correctly. But that may not be the case. I am not suggesting for a moment any sort of nihilism. But, for example, two people may look at a door. Both see it; they do not disagree that there is a door. Yet the meaning each gives the door, the way each thinks about the door, will vary tremendously from person to person, and from moment to moment. How can misperception occur when there is no objective meaning? From the standpoint of a paradigm shift, we may argue that the whole issue of perception is unimportant.

Deutsch argues that self-fulfilling prophecy is a source of conflict. If I say, 'I will be in conflict with you', and say it often enough, I may talk myself into that conflict. Yet that is a very simplistic notion of self-fulfilling prophecy. There are many Christians, for example, who believe in the Second Coming, and expect an end to the world, which will be preceded by a time of destruction. They may interpret events around them as being signs of that time of destruction. To take the point of view that conflict with Christians' eschatological perspective stems mostly from their self-fulfilling prophecy is to suggest that the way to resolve their conflict is to persuade them out of their beliefs. Would this really resolve the conflict? Would one be likely to persuade people out of their beliefs? Probably not. Again, a paradigm shift may lead the theorist to hold that self-fulfilling prophecies distract attention from the more fundamental theoretical questions.

To leave Deutsch aside, there is another illustration of conflict resolution without a paradigm shift found in rational choice theory, as especially represented by game theory. At its heart rational choice theory holds that individuals will make choices which are intended to maximize their payoffs and decrease their losses, and that parties 'know' what is best for themselves. Often, parties are said to be involved in games, or we might say negotiations, with others in order to seek a maximum payoff. Parties, however, may make mistakes throughout the games, often mistakes of perception. Nicholson (1991) has pointed out that there are three major sources of error in a player's game. Those types are, first, being ill-informed over the number and identity of actors in the conflict; second, having no knowledge of what the others want; and third, failure to understand the methods being used by the parties in obtaining their payoffs. Thus conflict resolution, from this perspective, would address itself to identifying the actors, increasing knowledge between the parties, and clarifying the methods being used to obtain payoffs.

Once again, though, we are faced with problems. There is no reason why identifying the relevant parties to a conflict will make resolution any easier; it could, in fact, make it more difficult. Generally speaking, more knowledge is better than less, but there are exceptions. For example, in a conflict over child custody, it may not necessarily be helpful to know that a friend is advising a former spouse. That kind of knowledge is often helpful in understanding conflict dynamics, but it also may escalate the conflict far beyond its current level.

Underlying many models of conflict resolution is the assumption that the major need in resolving conflict is information. In both Deutsch's and Nicholson's examples above, the primary goal of their approaches has been this: to increase knowledge. This, though, forces one to ask a question: knowledge about what? What kind of knowledge? If conflict is fundamentally a rational, intellectual process, then this may be a reasonable assumption. Yet conflict does not appear to be so rational or intellectual. If it were, then deterrence should work. Deterrence is predicated upon parties' knowing the costs of their behaviour, and therefore limiting what they do, in order not to incur those costs. Evidence abounds, though, that deterrence does not deter. No amount of information will persuade parties to avoid conflict.

Conclusion: Questions of Theory

Often the discussion of theory appears dry and unnecessary, especially to students of conflict resolution, who are, after all, interested in action. Yet it should be clear by now that theory is vital in any discussion of resolving conflict, inasmuch as it directs the researcher towards different kinds of questions. As was pointed out earlier, all behaviour is informed by theory; making those theories explicit, however, is vital for conflict resolution. Examination of theory also forces one to make clear one's assumptions about the value of conflict and about how the world works. If, at heart, one assumes rationality, then one will make choices along those lines in resolving conflict. If, on the other hand, rationality is not assumed, then different choices are made.

Each theorist mentioned above has made a significant contribution to the study of conflict resolution. Each also has faults, but that is inherent in the nature of theorizing. Some developed their theories without mentioning revolutions in science or paradigm shifts. These theorists were blazing a trail well within their disciplines. Simmel and Coser focused upon the positive value of conflict, noting that it has played a central role in forming the society in which we live. Lewin focused on two key themes: that resolving conflict is a value-laden enterprise; and that the practitioner of resolution, to be effective, must also be a theorist. These themes led to action research. Deutsch emphasized the role of the individual in conflict and examined the ways in which individual perceptions and biases influence conflict behaviour. Game theory raised the promise of being able to predict behaviour on the basis of rational analysis, and suggested that there were identifiable strategies available from which people could predict outcomes of given behaviour.

Other theorists wrote specifically of their revolutionary activity, rejecting the old assumptions and paradigms and replacing them with new ones. Burton is the best example of this rejection of the old for something new. His perspective is one wherein conflict cannot be understood in any limited sense, nor without considering the individuals' behaviour within a larger social context. Thus individual humans act to satisfy their needs, but they do it within a social context where the culture and resources of needs satisfaction are held collectively.

Common to all the theorists mentioned is the principle that communication plays a central role in conflict resolution. In the next chapter the well-worn topic of communication is considered, focusing on its influences both on the conduct of conflict and on the course of resolution.

References

Argyris, Christopher, Robert Putnam and Diana McLain Smith (1990) *Action Science*. San Francisco: Jossey-Bass.

Avruch, Kevin and Peter Black (1987) 'A Generic Theory of Conflict Resolution: A Critique', *Negotiation Journal* 2(1), 87–100.

Axelrod, Robert (1984) *The Evolution of Cooperation*. New York: Basic Books.

Burton, John (1979) *Deviance, Terrorism and War*. New York: St Martin's Press.

Burton, John (1993) 'From Strategic Deterrence to Problem Solving', in Kevin Clements (ed.), *Peace and Security in the Asia Pacific Region*. Tokyo: United Nations Press.

Burton, John and Dennis Sandole (1986) 'Generic Theory: The Basis of Conflict Resolution', *Negotiation Journal* 2(4), 333–44.

Coser, Lewis A. (1957) 'Social Conflict and Social Change', *British Journal of Sociology* 8(3), 197–207.

Coser, Lewis A. (1968) *The Functions of Social Conflict*. London: Routledge and Kegan Paul.

Deutsch, Morton (1973) *The Resolution of Conflict*. New Haven, CT: Yale University Press.

Deutsch, Morton (1991) 'Subjective Features of Conflict Resolution', in Raimo Väyrynen (ed.), *New Directions in Conflict Theory*. London: Sage.

Druckman, D., B. Broome and S. Korper (1988) 'Value Differences and Conflict Resolution: Facilitation or Delinking?', *Journal of Conflict Resolution* 32(3), 489–510.

Kuhn, Thomas S. (1970) *The Structure of Scientific Revolutions*. Chicago: University of Chicago Press.

Lewin, Kurt (1997) *Resolving Social Conflicts and Field Theory in Social Science*. Washington, DC: American Psychological Association.

Lippitt, Robert (1968) 'Kurt Lewin', in David L. Sills (ed.) *Encyclopedia of the Social Sciences*, vol. 9. New York: Macmillan.

Maslow, Abraham (1987) *Motivation and Personality*. New York: Harper and Row.

Nicholson, Michael (1991) 'Negotiation. Agreement and Conflict Resolution: The Role of Rational Approaches and Their Criticism', in Raimo Väyrynen (ed.), *New Directions in Conflict Theory*. London: Sage.

Northrup, Terrell A. (1989) 'The Dynamic of Identity in Personal and Social Conflict', in Louis Kriesberg, Terrell A. Northrup and Stuart J. Thorson (eds), *Intractable Conflicts and Their Transformation*. Syracuse, NY: Syracuse University Press.

Poundstone, William (1992) *Prisoner's Dilemma*. New York: Doubleday.

Pruitt, Dean G. and Peter J. Carnevale (1993) *Negotiation and Social Conflict*. London: Open University Press.

Sandole, Dennis (1993) 'Paradigms, Theories, and Metaphors in Conflict and Conflict Resolution: Coherence or Confusion?', in Dennis Sandole and Hugo van der Merwe (eds), *Conflict Resolution: Theory and Practice*. Manchester: Manchester University Press.

Simmel, Georg (1955) *Conflict and the Web of Group-Affiliations*. New York: The Free Press.

Sites, Paul (1973) *Control: The Basis of Social Order*. New York: Dunellen.

Väyrynen, Raimo (1991) 'To Settle or to Transform? Perspectives on the Resolution of National and International Conflicts', in Raimo Väyrynen (ed.), *New Directions in Conflict Theory*. London: Sage.

von Neumann, John and Oskar Morgenstern (1953) *Theory of Games and Economic Behavior*. Princeton, NJ: Princeton University Press.

Wallensteen, Peter (1991) 'The Resolution and Transformation of International Conflicts: A Structural Perspective', in Raimo Väyrynen (ed.), *New Directions in Conflict Theory*. London: Sage.

5
COMMUNICATION AND CONFLICT RESOLUTION

Introduction

Many, if not all, texts on conflict resolution address the importance of communication in the resolution of conflict. Communication is treated as a utilitarian device employed in pursuit of resolution. So, texts will address the relative merits of 'effective' communication in enhancing the resolution process. What these texts fail to do, by and large, is to focus on communication as an essential element of both conflict and its resolution. Communication is an essential ingredient to the prosecution of conflict between people, as much as it is a tool for resolving conflict.

A point of confusion surrounding communication resides in the very understanding of its nature. Imagine two negotiators in a room; one speaks Hebrew, the other Arabic. They speak to one another, but cannot comprehend the meaning that is intended. Some would say that the negotiators are failing to communicate; yet this would be a mistake. Communication indeed takes place, whether the two negotiators share a language or not. They have shared something very fundamental, even if they have not exchanged negotiation proposals: they have exchanged meaning with one another. What has not taken place is 'effective' communication. This is the point of departure for this chapter.

Communication plays a vital role in creating group solidarity, identifying the 'in-group' and the 'out-group'. It also serves as the basis of power: the distribution of power is often played out through communication. Even more fundamental than that, however, is the interaction between perception and language. This interaction impacts upon conflict in ways that may not be obvious to the casual observer. Therefore, communication plays a more subtle role in conflict than might be first appreciated.

Communication is the conduit of conflict, both for carrying out the fight and for gaining new supporters. Communication is also, of course, at the heart of the resolution process; without communication resolution cannot proceed. This last point often generates misunderstanding, however. While resolution requires communication, it is not true that good communication necessarily leads to resolution. In fact, a 'good' conflict is as dependent upon communication as is resolution. Underlying communication is the disposition of the parties; without the right disposition no amount of communication will suffice. Those disposed to resolving a conflict, or possessing the will to resolve, benefit more from and generate better communication than those who are of a competitive disposition (Deutsch, 1991). Whereas disposition influences the nature of communication, a key role that communication plays in conflict is to help classify the world into camps. An important way in which this is done is through the use of propaganda, which assists parties to galvanize support and carry out the conflict. Ultimately communication is a process through which parties may wield power, be it through propagating particular beliefs about the world or through classifying different parties in different ways.

In addressing these areas a general discussion is undertaken on the nature of communication and its features. Second, communication as a binding force is examined, one that links people, ideas and institutions together. But although there are ways in which communication binds people together, there are also ways in which it separates them. Quite wrongly, in some corners communication has won the title of saviour from conflict. This is a fallacious view. Therefore, communication as a divisive force, breaking relationships, ideas and institutions apart, is also examined. This last point is important, for many harbour the ill-founded idea that communication is purely a benevolent force. The idea of communication as being necessarily a binding force is fallacious, inasmuch as although communication can bring people together in harmony, it can also rip families, groups or nations asunder. It all depends upon what is communicated and how it is communicated. The racial hatred communicated and propagated by the Nazis in Germany's Third Reich serves as a shining example of just how dangerous and destructive communication can be. Equally, though, in cases where conflict has been effectively resolved communication has also played its role. How to use communication to resolve conflict will be left to other writers. The concern here is to examine how the ubiquitous nature of communication impacts upon all conflicts and all attempts at resolution.

Communication also has a direct impact upon the three necessary and sufficient conditions of conflict resolution. First, the capacity to resolve may be influenced by the ability to coordinate activity among group members, such as the members of a labour bargaining unit or a social group. Coordination is governed by the ability to communicate. Second, while opportunities to resolve may be had, they are often created by communicating with others and informing them and persuading them of the existence of such opportunities. Finally, the volition to resolve is often created through communication, and is certainly often discovered through communication.

Some Observations about Communication

'You cannot not communicate' is an oft-heard refrain among those who study communication. That you cannot not communicate, or that people always communicate as long as they are engaged in thought, may need some explaining. A negotiator speaking Arabic, for example, may be engaged with a counterpart who is speaking Hebrew – and neither speaks any other language. While each may be eloquent in their own tongue, neither will foster the meaning they intend in the mind of the other. Each may believe the other to be speaking about peace in the Middle East, though each may be discussing an excellent recipe for chicken. The quality of the communication one receives resides largely in the head of the receiver, and the meaning of that communication depends, to a large extent, on what the receiver believes it to be.

It would be foolhardy, though, to suggest that we live in a world where the totality of meaning is created in our heads alone. Clearly, we share a degree of meanings, and this is an important point of departure: the meanings we share create bonds between us and divisions as well. The bonds are created because those with whom we share meaning have similar perspectives on the world; they see many of the same things that we do. Those with whom we do not share meaning, however, are apart from us, and difficult to communicate with. We may even castigate, vilify and oppose those with whom we do not share meaning.

The ubiquitous nature of communication leads any study of human interaction to the necessity of understanding how communication impacts upon that interaction. Two areas of interest in the study of conflict are judgement and motivation. Brehmer (1988) correctly comments, though, that both judgement and motivation are hidden from view; they cannot be observed. Through communication people may gain some understanding about how people make judgements and what motivates them.

One central area of concern here is the nexus between communication and conflict.

Communication and Conflict

Most conflict relies upon communication for its externalization. Many conflicts that might otherwise remain in the hearts and minds of the parties become manifest when those parties communicate. Question: how do we know when a conflict exists? Answer: because somebody told us. Through communication we express, intentionally or otherwise, our conflict experiences. We discover others' conflict experiences through communication. Even if someone in conflict does not consciously report the existence of a conflict, the conflict may still become expressed. Even unmanifest conflict will impact on the social settings, in that it influences the behaviours of those in that relationship. Accepted social inequity may be an example of unmanifest conflict. The party of lesser status may not make public statements about the inequity even if they do in fact feel quite wronged.

Before we move on, a definition of communication is in order. Communication can be defined as the exchange of meaning. It is process oriented, and ongoing. Communication does not operate in a discrete and staccato manner of input then output, *ad infinitum*. Rather it is a continuous process of simultaneous and seamless inputs and outputs. Most important in communication is symbolization. Symbols act in lieu of something else; they stand for something. The words 'I love you' stand for my inner state, my affective disposition towards you. The words also carry the message that the speaker is a symbol-using animal, and understands, at least on some level, the principles of English grammar, and is enculturated within a culture that has some access to a given language.

The power of symbolizing, be it speaking, writing, drawing, making hand gestures, or using cultural artefacts (e.g. knives and guns), makes plain the existence of conflict. People know that a conflict exists, too, because the symbols used to express it are in a form that is understood. Most such symbols are culturally contextual: that is, we learn their meaning from the enculturation process we went through. Some symbols, though, may be less cultural and more generically human. A screaming session between two people (where both shake their fists and are red in the face), it may be argued, would be identified everywhere as a fight. Interpretations might vary as to just how intense a fight it was, or whether it was acceptable, but virtually everybody would see it as a fight. So, in this sense, there may be a few symbols which are universal, albeit abstract and vague.

Yet most conflict is influenced profoundly in its expression by culture. There are some universal principles that can be brought to bear on the discussion of conflict and communication. Perhaps the most important of any universal in the discussion of conflict and communication is the use of the negative. All people are symbol-using creatures, and to that end, all people make symbols to describe or stand for something. That thing, of course, need not be a physical object; the thing can be the figment of someone's very active imagination. The point is that all people use symbols. While symbols stand for things, they also stand for 'not-things': that is, things which are not there. All symbols refer to things, but in so doing also stand for things that they are not. So, the word banana refers to yellow, curved fruit. It also stands for not-orange, not-apple, not-car, not-poison. As Burke (1966) argued, humans are the 'inventor of the negative'. Along with symbol using comes the capacity to discuss that which is 'not'. Burke (ibid., p. 10) adds:

> For the negative is but a *principle*, an *idea*, not a name for a *thing*. And thus, whereas an injunction such as 'thou shalt not kill' is understandable enough, as a negative *idea*, it also has about its edges the positive *image* of killing. But the main point is: Though a child may not always obey the 'thou shalt not,' and though there may inevitably be, in the offing, an image positively inviting disobedience, the child 'gets the idea.'

The power of the negative is clear, and has obvious efficacy in any human interaction.

One of the key aspects of the negative comes in the human ability to classify. As Hodge and Kress (1993, p. 62) note, 'Classification is at the basis of language and thought.' Through classification we organize and arrange the world into a meaningful whole. Thus we can talk of dogs, cats, friends, families, allies, enemies, and so on. Each of these classifications, as you might note, concerns conflict. We use classification to separate ourselves from those with whom we are in conflict.

The manner in which people classify, though, is debatable. There are those who argue that there is an inherent guide to classification. Chomsky (quoted in Maratsos, 1979, p. 246) argues, 'Human beings are specially designed to acquire language, with data-handling or hypothesis-formulating ability of unknown character and complexity.' The source of our linguistic ability is biologically determined, so the argument would go, to some extent. Thus all people classify a dog as separate and different from a tree. Chomsky's observation places both language and classification as inherent human behaviours. Furthermore, if Chomsky is right, then we all have the ability to test the validity of our classifications, by formulating hypotheses.

Thus while there may be a level at which our classifications are biologically influenced, by virtue of the structures of our brains, there is still a high level of plasticity in classification. This plasticity comes from the ability to use the negative. We can always say what something is not; there are an infinite number of things which something is not. In conflict resolution, at its most simplistic, anybody can move from saying 'he is my not-friend' to 'he is not my enemy'. The challenge for conflict resolution is to find a way in which needs can be satisfied, so that those in conflict no longer say, 'I am not secure', but 'I am secure.' The challenge, furthermore, is that there are an infinite number ways in which a party may find their security tested. Challenges to security, like so much of communication, can be found in the perceptions of individuals and groups of the world around them.

Perception

Perception simply refers to the way in which an individual interprets the world. As social actors we constantly 'decode' messages from the world around us. The codes we break, however, are not written in stone; we decode messages according to our internal standards. There may be social methods for decoding a message, such as a grammar, but grammars do not tell us what meaning to give to a certain message. So, I might hear someone say, 'It's a beautiful day', but is there a guarantee how I will react to that message? Will I be pleased? I might not be pleased if I am working inside all day. Will I agree? If the speaker meant a beautiful day because it is raining and there has been a drought, I may not agree; I still may prefer sunshine.

The Sapir–Whorf hypothesis contends that language structures reality. The classic example is of the Inuit people, who have several words for snow, while in Western European culture we have only one. European descriptions of snow would fall far short of the Inuits' needs, whereas most Europeans would find the Inuit descriptions excessive and unnecessary. Listening to the way others speak tells much about the way they see the world. Also, language influences the ways in which people see the world. Consider the folk saying, 'Either you're for me, or you're against me.' This presents an absolute sense of friend and enemy. There is no in-between ground.

Clearly, perception has an important role to play in conflict resolution. Person A's perception of B's behaviour may not reflect A's intentions. In this simple way, much of conflict resolution may focus on clarifying these perceptions. As was stated in the preceding chapter, however, it is important not to assume that clarifying perceptions is the main task of conflict resolution. Rather, understanding the process of perception and its impact on social settings is more appropriate to conflict resolution. One important aspect of perception, for example, is its collective nature. People do not create their perceptions in a vacuum. Everybody is influenced in their perceptions by the collective force of the groups around them. Furthermore, perception cannot be turned off, and it is here that the phrase 'you cannot not communicate' is played out, because as long as one perceives, one is decoding meaning, thereby communicating. Through social interaction and communication we divide the world up into different categories, and perceive each category differently from each other.

Perception creates individuality and difference; yet perception also ties us together in some interesting ways. For example, there are some predictable ways in which perceptions become skewed. Behavioural decision theory casts an interesting light on the ways in which perceptions influence decision-making behaviour. People use heuristic devices to simplify decisions in the light of their perceptions, especially when those people perceive situations with a degree of uncertainty. Uncertainty, of course, can exist when decisions are complex, or there is incomplete information. Although heuristics simplify judgement and decision-making in the face of uncertainty, they also sometimes result in bad or incorrect decisions.

Kahneman and Tversky (1982) identified three heuristics commonly used by people: representativeness, anchoring and availability. *Representativeness* refers to events where the perceived probability of the occurrence of an event is based upon a given event's similarity to another event. For example, assume that you meet Cathy, who is tall, thin and pale of complexion, wears thick glasses and is very quiet. You are asked to predict what she does for a living. Is she a librarian, exotic dancer or airline pilot? Typically, most would predict that Cathy is a librarian because of her physical similarity to what librarians 'should' look like. As Saks and Kidd (1988, p. 221) note, however, 'judging the probability of an event based on its similarity to or representativeness of other events may lead to defects in judgement'. Individuals in conflict often mistakenly collate two or more conflicts together under one descriptive heading and use one resolution method for all these conflicts. The result is often that a resolution strategy may work for one conflict but fail in others.

A second type of heuristic is *anchoring* (Saks and Kidd, 1988, pp. 228–9):

> To illustrate the anchoring principle two groups of high school students were given one of two problems to solve. One group was asked to estimate, without aid of paper and pencil, the product of the following sequence:
>
> $$8 \times 7 \times 6 \times 5 \times 4 \times 3 \times 2 \times 1 = ?$$
>
> The other group was asked to estimate the product of these same numbers presented in ascending order.
>
> Usually the students simply multiplied together the first two or three numbers and then extrapolated from this product to the final guess. If this is indeed how they performed the calculations to arrive at a final product, then the anchoring principle should have caused the first, descending group to judge the final product as larger than the second, ascending group.

The type of information and the manner in which it is presented influence the way in which people will make judgements about a given event. Anchoring has clear implications for negotiation behaviour, for example, because parties must often make snap decisions based upon information presented by somebody else. A skilful negotiator will present information in such a way that the anchoring principle will work in his or her interest.

The third heuristic is *availability*, which occurs when 'people are likely to judge the probability or frequency of an event based upon the ease with which they can recall instances or occurrences of the event' (Saks and Kidd, 1988, p. 225). Obviously, recent events are more likely to be viewed as likely to repeat themselves than events from the distant and often unmemorable past. The manner in which we recall the past, however, is not totally left up to us. Groups, societies and cultures often provide methods by which we are reminded of events, so that they are kept in the forefront of our minds. Nationalist holidays are just one such example of how the set of available events from which to draw inferences may be manipulated.

What these heuristics suggest is that there are predictable and stable ways in which people make incorrect inferences from environmental data. People perceive the world around them and make decisions about likely or unlikely events. The reliability of those predictions, however, can often be called into question. Although heuristic devices often provide people with quick and correct insights from which to make decisions, they may also mislead. The importance of the behavioural decision-making school to the study of conflict and conflict resolution is quite clear. People in conflict use these heuristics to assist in decision-making processes. Attempts at resolution may be thwarted by poor decision-making, affected by the use of these judgement heuristics.

A caveat is worth adding regarding perception. What people perceive is not necessarily objectively so, nor is it even necessarily rational. Take, for example, intuition. People often have a sense of something about to happen, either good or bad, which leads to changes in behaviour. Jung defined intuition as 'a perception, by ways or means of the unconscious' (quoted in Evans, 1966, p. 100). What we perceive may, in fact, be buried well within our psyche and only bubble out occasionally in the form of intuition. As a source of information, intuitive information is very powerful, but also difficult to communicate. Intuitions represent another input into the process of judgement, but they seem badly accounted for in much of the literature on conflict resolution. From this brief discussion of perception it seems apparent that there are many influences on the way in which we judge our environment. Some of those influences are obvious and easily accounted for, others are far more difficult to grapple with. The remainder of this chapter focuses on communication and the social context.

Group Communication

The study of perception more often than not focuses on how an individual processes the world at large. Yet there are other approaches to the study of communication, including an examination of the process of how groups interact and are influenced by communication. A group can be defined as any collectivity of people, numbering more than three persons, who consciously share some common beliefs and who come together with some common purpose in mind. That is, a group is a purposeful thing, and not simply a crowd. A gaggle of people waiting on a street corner is not a group because they do not consciously share common goals or common beliefs. Yet the 'Nation of Israel' (Jews in Israel and members of the diaspora) is a group, inasmuch as they consciously share common beliefs.

All groups have members of varying dedication to the group itself. Some members are highly motivated and see the group as central to them, whereas others are less motivated. Regardless of the degree of motivation, though, the group affects all members. It influences choices people make, the language they use and the beliefs they hold. The communication an individual experiences in a group is very different from that, say, of a duo. Two people talking quietly in a corner of a bar have some very different kinds of interactions as compared with members of a group. Groups evolve norms and rules, which individuals will follow. Recall Milgram's experiments, where individuals issued pseudo-shocks, believing them to be real shocks, to confederates in the experiment. Under social pressure and expectations, individuals were observed to issue would-be near-lethal doses of electricity. This kind of conformance to authority has salience for group behaviour, where individuals will undertake behaviour that they normally would forego. The most obvious example can be found in the armed services, where group pressure and norms transform normally peaceable individuals into soldiers and trained killers.

Regardless of the group's nature, there are two fundamental functions that must be addressed: maintenance and task. A maintenance function refers to the upkeep of the group, maintaining moral, group service, group identity. This is a care-taking function of the group, and is important in the group's longevity. The task function of a group refers to that which the group is intended to do. A group that comes together to worship God has a task function of religious reverence. Group energy, however, is finite; groups cannot expend energy on one function without withdrawing energy from another function. So, groups cannot spend all of their time on the one function and still have time left for maintaining the group.

Not only do all groups share this division between task and maintenance, but also all groups possess leaders. Within any group there is a division between individuals, meaning that some individuals are helping to guide the group towards some collective end. Of course, leadership is not limited to charismatic types. More often than not when leadership is mentioned most people think in terms of a person with a strong character, good speaking voice and powerful presence who commands group attention. Such a person, however, is in reality rare, and even when present may not be a particularly important leader. A leader is any person who guides a group towards collective goals. That person may not be charismatic at all, but may in fact be quite quiet, shy, small in stature and with a host of other unassuming features. Furthermore, leaders are rarely formally recognized. Some leaders hold leadership titles, such as president, manager, chief executive, but others hold no formal title of leadership. A characteristic of leaders is that they use the discourse of leadership. They speak for the group, using discourse patterns and symbols reflecting group values and norms. Leaders may also attempt to give the group new values and norms, but even in the most authoritarian of groups members must still legitimize the use of those terms.

Communication, Classification and Groups

Communication and language, specifically, provides the reflection of how we divide the world into groups. Most obviously, the world is divided into groups who speak a common language and those who do not. There is the group called Anglophones (hence Winston Churchill's *History of the English-Speaking Peoples*), others called Francophones, Sinophones, and so on. These are the formal languages by which people are separated, and these language groups often, though not always, also correspond to cultural groups. Yet language is further used to separate people and to create new groupings. Giles and Coupland (1991) argue there is an important link between social identity and self-concept, and that our social identity relies upon separating our social group favourably from other groups. Thus

> This process of achieving positive distinctiveness enables individuals to achieve a satisfactory social identity and thereby enhances their own positive self-esteem. When ethnic identity becomes important for individuals, they may attempt to make themselves favourably distinct on dimensions such as language. (ibid., p. 105)

Take, for example, African Americans, who share with a majority of other Americans the use of English as their first language. Yet by the very label 'African Americans' we can already see the separation of one group from another. This separation, though, is not in name only, but also reflected in language. There is recognition that among many African Americans there is a language which is used, often termed 'Black American English'. It has historical antecedents which make it different from the language spoken by, for example, an Italian American. The linguistic differences, though, are not simply accidents of history. Rather, they serve an explicit political and organizational purpose. Language creates a sense of identity and oneness, a sense of group identity and belonging. Parallels can be found throughout the world where groups have sought for one reason or another to separate themselves from other groups, and have created a sense of group identity.

The operation of language as a mark of identity, however, works at an even more basic level. Not only is there the sense of ethnic identity, but there is that of simple group identity as well. The use of 'in' language denotes membership in a group. Hall (1981, p. 132) argues that 'there is no such thing as a basic form of the language that is universally applicable'. Instead, people develop situation dialects, each employed in different situations, such as in the presence of a group. One need only think about one's workplace to find examples of language as membership. Office routines have specific names unique to that office. One of the great challenges in changing jobs is picking up quickly and efficiently the new vocabulary. Try, sometime, to use non-routine language in your place of employment; you will note peculiar looks, or even outright 'corrections'. Once again, these are examples of situational language reflecting the dividing up of the world into groups.

There are countless examples of language acting as the source of conflict. Virtually anywhere in the USA today you can create an argument by discussing bilingual education. Native English speakers may rebel against an education system that offers education in both English and some other language. Equally, non-native English speakers may rebel against bilingualism, arguing that it prevents one from 'becoming an American'. In the workplace some words may be taboo. For example, in some workplaces the word 'problem' is proscribed, and replaced with far milder terms such as 'challenge'. Elsewhere throughout the world the issue of language has generated tremendous conflicts. The explosion of violence in Soweto, South Africa, in 1976 grew out of a decision by the state government to educate all black children in Afrikaans. The children protested, then the police attacked, and there ensued a bloody conflict, resulting in hundreds of casualties. Which language you speak can present itself as a source of considerable motivation to action.

Hodge and Kress (1993) make the point that language often separates us from what we are not, thus there is born an anti-language. An anti-language serves 'to transform what is troublesome and problematic in reality into something less disturbing, something homely and harmless. ... An anti-language is a device for managing reality, creating the necessary counter reality' (ibid., p. 72). Anti-language makes heroic that which is only moderately good, or that which may be seen by others as explicitly negative. Anti-language also makes evil that which is valued by the opposition. An example of the action of an anti-language is found, again, in African American language. The expression 'bad' meaning that which is 'cool' (itself anti-language) or good is an excellent example of anti-language: 'He's bad' is a popular expression meaning 'he's cool'. As the popular culture image, as portrayed in film and elsewhere, continues to vilify the young male African American, there is a demand for a reply. The vilification of young African American men clearly demands a reply – turning the logic of vilification on its head, thus, 'he's bad'. Anti-language is negation at its most powerful and effective.

Not only does this language serve to mark the identity of its user, it can often be used to increase that user's security. Knowing the grammar of a given anti-language insulates and protects its users. They are able to insulate themselves against interlopers. Security is sought and sometimes obtained by the knowledge that the language is 'special' and unique, and that its users are uniquely qualified to use it. Secret societies, whether employing anti-language or not, may use secret codes and passwords to indicate those who are part of the group, as opposed to those outside. In this way, it appears that there is a strong linguistic feature in the formation and protection of groups.

The formation of groups is not solely a linguistic event, though it is certainly reflected in language. Groups are an everyday given in human life. We are all members of groups, including family, work, neighbourhood, school, university, recreational, class, ethnicity, religion and nation. The origin of group membership is debatable, and reflects many of the issues found in inherency, contingency and interactionist theories. Is our membership due to our social learning, some fundamental drive, or some combination of the two?

Social learning theories suggest that our reliance on groups grows out of our very early learning about group life, as we were raised within a family. From these familial settings has grown our entire group life. Social comparison theory holds that people have a strong desire to compare their behaviour, well-being and actions with those of others. In order to do this, people exist in groups, so that they may obtain information about themselves, thus heightening their ability to improve and protect themselves (Baron *et al.*, 1993). A third set of theories are exchange theories, wherein people see relationships as exchanges of profits and losses. Social relationships and groups are formed in order to facilitate the acquisition of social goods, which in themselves foster individual security.

Many theories of the group rely upon functional explanations. Usually, functionalist explanations rest upon the observation that groups are collectively better at problem-solving than individuals. They are better than individuals because groups possess more information, and more minds with which to think about the problem. In group studies this collective aspect of the group is known as 'synergy': the whole is greater than the sum of the parts. The difficulty, of course, with functionalist theories is that they presume that people collect in groups for survival or socially competitive reasons. It is always possible that people form themselves into groups for no particular reason at all. If people do form groups for a reason, then what might those reasons be? Below is a list of some possibilities.

- mate selection
- security
- identity
- to engage in conflict
- for defence
- to increase the effective use of resources
- for fun
- inertia – people are born into groups, why leave?

Whatever the reasons for our group-centredness, it remains clear that our language reflects our reliance upon groups and classification. People announce daily their group identity, and the manner in which they divide the world.

Propaganda, Public Opinion and Conflict

Propaganda and the creation and manipulation of public opinion are widespread, and present in almost all conflicts. There are very few conflicts that exist in which some party or other is not trying to influence an audience of potential supporters about the nature of the conflict. In essence all conflicts operate on at least two planes:

between the parties and between each party and the outside world. Much attention has been paid to the former, but often not enough to the latter. In some conflicts explanations and rationalizations of conflicts are highly ritualized, whereas in others they must be invented.

Propaganda and the formation of a 'public opinion' are not things that only states do. Often we speak of something as being 'mere' propaganda, but this is a mistake. Propaganda is around us every day; we use it all the time, and engage in its creation daily. It has special relevance in any discussion of social and structural conflict. At its most basic, propaganda is the propagation or creation of an idea or opinion where none existed before. It is used to create a 'public', though a public may be created without the purposeful use of propaganda. People may coalesce around an event, all holding an opinion about the event, without any outside agency trying to create opinion. A tornado going through a town is an event around which opinion may form without any propaganda effort. On the other hand, industrial layoffs form the basis upon which propaganda efforts emerge from both the employees and the employers.

A public may be defined as a group who are inclined to act in similar ways in relation to some event or stimulus. Lippmann (1946, p. 20) argued that

> Those features of the world outside which have to do with the behavior of other human beings, in so far as that behavior crosses ours, or is interesting to us, we call roughly public affairs. The pictures inside the heads of those human beings, the pictures of themselves, of others, of their needs, purposes, and relationship, are their public opinions.

Publics are created, in part, out of language and the process of classification. Linguistically, classifications are made which delineate one set of opinion from another. 'Slogans' become the public labels determining the set of opinion to which one belongs. 'I Like Ike' signals who your presidential choice is, and says something to others about the kinds of classifications you make for yourself. People will interact on the basis of these classifications, and the perception of their validity. Thus the creation of a public can be seen to be an action that carries with it a social meaning. We can speak of 'publics', such as those who favour the availability of abortion and those who do not.

The formation of a public occurs around issues, but may also form around needs satisfiers, beliefs, values, or other such public items. An example of the formation of public opinion will suffice. Public opinion formed around the decision to go to war is based upon a set of focal areas around which opinion may be stirred. The leadership of a group, either formal or informal, will articulate a series of statements that reflect group values that relate those values to the decision for war. At the outset of the Gulf War the US government articulated a variety of reasons, including the protection of the nation-state system, defence of an ally, opposition to 'naked aggression', and protection of the oil supply, to name a few. One's opinion regarding these issues determined one's relationship to the leadership of the group, and the rest of the group as a whole. Strong opposition to the 'group' opinion could well have led to individuals' being virtually exiled from that group. This has always been the case with anti-war protesters, in that they are quickly vilified and ousted from the group. During the 1960s Vietnam era the bumper sticker 'America, Love It or Leave It' amply demonstrated the power of propaganda and group membership. Ultimately, it is the use of public discourse and utterances related to behaviour that determine one's position *vis-à-vis* the group. That position also determines one's access to group resources. Clearly, if the group possesses resources vital for life, then opposition to the group position is unlikely.

Propaganda, of course, can be used to empower a group and build its membership. Not only, then, does propaganda have a negative aspect, in that it can be used to oust marginal members, but it can also have a positive aspect, wherein it attracts new members. For example, there may be a workplace conflict focusing on work practices. The issue may upset only a small number of people. Their propaganda may be uniquely focused on denouncing management. Although the opposing group may have only a small number of adherents, the leadership may come to decide that their numbers need to be increased. The group may therefore change its propaganda tactics, away from the vilification of management and towards attracting new members. This new focus does not, however, suggest that the group is no longer willing to vilify management; it may simply be making a tactical choice. As it gains new followers, and its human resources grow, the group may then be in a better position to oppose management.

Propaganda is used by individuals, groups, organizations and states to propagate, or create, an idea or association where none existed before. Lenin offers an illustration: 'The propagandist dealing with, say, the question of unemployment, must explain the capitalist nature of the crisis, the causes of their inevitability in modern society' (quoted in Kenez, 1985). Propaganda in this example occurs when the propagandist acts in such a way as to make explicit a connection that may not have existed before. This, too, happens in conflict behaviour and is part of the process of classification. The propagandist provides the basis upon which new classifications can occur, thus creating new groups, or adding strength to existing groups. It is important to note, however, that propaganda occurs over a continuum of purposiveness. That is to say, some propaganda is designed and created in order to yield a particular political outcome. Other propaganda may be less forthright in its intention. In fact, the intention of some propaganda may be ill-defined and poorly articulated. Thus it is useful to think of propaganda along a continuum of purposiveness (see Figure 5.1).

Propaganda, however, is not something that is particularly new to any human conduct. Any parent who speaks lovingly, and with implied superiority, of his or her own children is a propagandist. Humans, to have their needs met, will propagate certain views of the world. This is an important point, inasmuch as needs may be biological, yet they are satisfied within a social context. Needs may not, generally, be satisfied without the cooperation of other members of a given group. Therefore, persuasion and propaganda operate to build collectives of individuals and groups which support a given

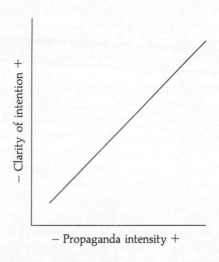

Figure 5.1 Intensity of propaganda in relation to the clarity of its purpose

needs satisfaction behaviour. Clark (1993) argues that cultures arise in order to satisfy human needs, and evolve over time. Each culture, then, will possess stories which explain their origins, and define who that group is. Eliade (1975) notes that cultures also develop stories of themselves, and explanations for their origins, often termed myths, and that these myths are often recounted. It is not a distant link that joins propaganda and the myth. The myth becomes a tool which binds the group together, explains its being, and classifies its members in some way.

These explanations, stories, myths and methods of classification reflect 'worldviews', or ways in which we see the world. A worldview is not too different from a paradigm, and the two words are often used interchangeably. All groups possess a collective worldview, which consists, among other things, of methods for satisfying human needs. Yet as Clark (1993, p. 35) points out 'Not *all* [emphasis original] worldviews, no matter how loyally defended, are equally satisfying of human needs.' Some worldviews may portray needs satisfaction as if basic human needs were in scarce supply. For example, the need for identity may be satisfied through a worldview that limits the number of possible group participants. Where identity is obtained through national citizenship, this need is seen as scarce indeed, and distributed selectively and sparingly in many states. Immigrants, would-be members of the state/group, must pass through various tests, all of which are designed to weed out 'undesirable' potential group members. To this extent, then, national citizenship as a satisfier of identity is seen as scarce.

It is important to remember, though, that propaganda is fluid and flexible. Often, what one believes to be a hard and fast rule of society turns out to be propaganda. This does not mean it is not powerful, but rather that it is elastic and subject to change. For example, the Israeli government has often announced that it would not negotiate with terrorists. The PLO, which had been responsible for acts of terrorism, would, under this Israeli pledge, never be invited to negotiate. Yet events in 1993 and 1994 proved this wrong; the propaganda changed and gave way to a new line. The Israeli government would never negotiate with terrorists, except for the PLO, which in turn renounced the use of terrorism as a political tool. The rigid rule gives way to the exigencies of reality; 'never' becomes 'sometimes'. This has also proven to be true in the case of the British government and the IRA.

The process of employing propaganda arguments is universal, and found in virtually every conflict. There are ritualized explanations for

why the conflict exists, why groups do what they do. Equally, there
are arguments that explain why needs are satisfied in the way that
they are. Perhaps the most telling area where communication,
language and propaganda are expressed is in the use of history.

The Power of Language

It should be clear that there is considerable interest in the nature, use
and type of language among groups. Who uses what types of language in order to engage in what type of social interaction is of the
utmost concern to any group and its members. Many groups
prohibit the use of various kinds of discourse in an effort to maintain
control. Discourse calling for the overthrow of a government is
proscribed in many nation-states, both because of the real danger
that somebody might actually try to overthrow a government, and
also because it represents a symbolic challenge to the legitimacy of a
given government. Any group possesses an ideology, which can be
defined as a body of discourse that explains the existence and
objectives of a given group. Ideology serves an important purpose,
inasmuch as it helps guide and govern the group in question. It also
rarely appears to be 'ideological', inasmuch as that ideology usually
comes in the guise of common sense. Americans will announce they
have freedom of speech, and that it just makes sense that freedom of
speech is good. This is ideology, yet most Americans would not
recognize it as such.

All groups, regardless of political hue, have an ideology. Yet
ideology is also power, and resides mainly in the leadership of a
given group. Fairclough (1992, p. 33) argues that 'Ideological power,
the power to project one's practice as universal and "common sense",
is a significant complement to economic and political power.'

Language, however, is not stable; it is dynamic and always
moving, as is ideology. The ideological centre of a group is always in
flux, and it is ever-changing because of the behaviour of the
individual members of the group. Individuals are, at heart, their own
kind of politicians, always on the move, ready to win new followers.
This is the case because people want to get their way, they want
their view of the world to prevail, if for no other reason than it is
theirs. Lakoff (1990, p. 18) argues:

> We may enter the [communication] transaction knowingly or not, we
> may function mainly as manipulator or manipulatee – but we are always
> involved in persuasion, in trying to get another person to see the world

or some piece of it our way, and therefore to act as we would like them to act. If we succeed, we have power.

The inescapable conclusion is that language and communication are power. To be powerful is not only to carry a gun, but to be able to exclude others from resources, both real and symbolic, and this is done through language. It is also the ability to coordinate activity, which is also carried out by communication and language. Most power, it seems, wielded in this world is linguistic and communicative. All communication events, including the speeches, the quiet chats, the books written and the hand gestures, all are moments where the potential to wield power exists.

Conclusion: The Language and Conflict Nexus

Language and communication are equally important in conflict and its resolution. In either case they serve a central role of coordinating action, of serving as a conduit through which individuals are linked to ideas, and as a method for wielding power. In cases of conflict there can be little doubt that people fight over words. The insulted party in some idealized eighteenth-century European setting duelling to clear his honour is not too far from reality today. Language is a reason to fight, as is so amply illustrated in the case of the Soweto riots mentioned. Burton may theorize that conflict occurs when needs go unsatisfied, yet the satisfaction of needs depends largely upon language to coordinate social activity in order that those needs may be satisfied. Deutsch's emphasis on perception and its role in conflict focuses our attention on the way in which language and communication can misrepresent or skew our perception of events. Communication and language play a central role in most forms of conflict resolution behaviour, including negotiation, mediation and facilitation. These practices essentially rely upon an individual to alter their symbolic environment, prior to altering their physical one.

It is true that communication plays a central role in conflict and its resolution, and it is also true that texts on conflict resolution are generally correct to emphasize the positive value of good communication. It is also worth acknowledging the much larger role communication plays. Analysts of conflict and practitioners of conflict resolution must be equally aware of how communication and language influence the process of conflict and its resolution. One fact remains: there can be no societal conflict without communication, just as there can be no societal resolution of that conflict without communication.

There appear to be some universal aspects to communication, including the facts that all people perceive, all perceptions are only reflections of the outer world, and all people communicate. While these universals have an impact on the process of conflict and its resolution, it is also important to note that conflict and conflict resolution are equally influenced by more elastic processes. The formation of groups and the creation and use of power through language serve as reminders of ways in which communication must be understood.

References

Baron, Robert S., Norbert Kerr and Norman Miller (1993) *Group Process, Group Decision, Group Action*. London: Open University Press.

Brehmer, Berndt (1988) 'The Role of Judgment in Small-Group Conflict and Decision Making', in Hal R. Arkes and Kenneth R. Hammond (eds), *Judgment and Decision Making*. Cambridge: Cambridge University Press.

Burke, Kenneth (1966) *Language as Symbolic Action*. Los Angeles: University of California Press.

Clark, Mary (1993) 'Symptoms of Cultural Pathologies: A Hypothesis', in Dennis Sandole and Hugo van der Merwe (eds), *Conflict Resolution: Theory and Practice*. Manchester: Manchester University Press.

Deutsch, Morton (1991) 'Subjective Features of Conflict Resolution', in Raimo Väyrynen (ed.), *New Directions in Conflict Theory*. London: Sage.

Eliade, Mircea (1975) *Myth and Reality*. New York: Harper Colophon Books.

Evans, Richard I. (1966) *Jung on Elementary Psychology*. New York: E.P. Dutton and Co.

Fairclough, Michael (1992) *Language as Power*. New York: Longman.

Giles, Howard and Nikolas Coupland (1991) *Language: Contexts and Consequences*. Milton Keynes: Open University Press.

Hall, Edward T. (1981) *Beyond Culture*. Garden City, NY: Anchor Books.

Hodge, Robert and Gunther Kress (1993) *Language as Ideology*. London: Routledge.

Kahneman, Daniel and Amos Tversky (1982) 'Judgement under Uncertainty: Heuristics and Biases', in *Judgement under Uncertainty*. Cambridge: Cambridge University Press.

Kenez, Peter (1985) *The Birth of the Propaganda State*. Cambridge: Cambridge University Press.

Lakoff, Robin Tolmach (1990) *Talking Power*. Basic Books.

Lippmann, Walter (1946) *Public Opinion*. New York: Pelican Books.

Saks, Michael J. and Robert F. Kidd (1988) 'Human Information Processing and Adjudication: Trial by Heuristics', in Hal R. Arkes and Kenneth R. Hammond (eds), *Judgment and Decision Making*. Cambridge: Cambridge University Press.

6
HISTORY AND CONFLICT RESOLUTION

Introduction: The Place of History

The place of history in the conduct and understanding of conflict and conflict resolution is a much understudied field. Historical studies, in and of themselves, have found a place in many studies of conflict, but these have been contained within the various disciplines, such as industrial relations, political science and international relations. These studies are highly specific to the given conflict event and description, yet reflect little integration into the corpus of conflict resolution. There are few who have written much about the role of history in conflict, despite the fact that history plays a vital and even a central role in the process of conflict and conflict resolution.

For a third party, such as a mediator, ignoring history in conflict is like ignoring a fault line running through the centre of a city: you can build on it, the city might even last for a while, but eventually it will fall down. In past studies of conflict resolution there has been a considerable emphasis on participant behaviour, examining conflict strategy and the selection of options. These studies have been most useful, as far as they have gone. What they have not done, however, is provide adequate explanations as to why and how actors come to the choices they make. For example, Simon (1986) has suggested that bounded rationality is one explanation of human decision-making. Bounded rationality means that people make choices based upon limited information, and will make decisions that are 'good enough', but far from optimal. Yet when entering a conflict situation it is not enough simply to know that actors will make decisions that they believe 'good enough'. Rather, third parties and researchers must know where to focus their attention. History provides third parties and researchers with direction, as it also provides explanations for actors' motivations.

Blake and Mouton believe that history has both a positive and a negative role in conflict resolution. They argue:

> On the positive side, a group's history provides its members with continuity and stability — an anchor in time and space. History helps group members understand where they are and how they got there. Records of the past are useful to group members in charting growth and development and in establishing important patterns and trends. (Blake and Mouton, 1984, pp. 3–4)

On the negative side, however, they see history as creating barriers to conflict resolution:

> History limits a group's vision of future alternatives and possibilities to those that individuals believe other members will understand, approve and accept. Past experiences, distorted by time and tainted by subjectivity, are characteristically accepted as valid predictors of the group's response to various suggestions. Recommendations that are contrary to history may be summarily dismissed, and the individual who proposed them may be censured or temporarily rejected. (Ibid., p. 4)

In sum, conflict resolution can be made profoundly difficult because of history's 'power over thought, feelings, and action' (ibid., p. 4).

The purpose of this chapter is twofold. First, it aims to provide a general overview of the ways in which history can impact upon conflict and conflict resolution. Historical memories offer explanations for future activities, and guide future events. They also proscribe certain alternatives that, if taken, might go a long way towards undoing a particular conflict. A historical perspective influences the judgement of parties to conflict, limiting, curtailing and creating options for behaviour. It is also a window into motivation, and the rationale behind choices made. The second purpose of the chapter is to provide an idea of how the study of history might offer some insight into a conflict and assist the analyst in its resolution.

History, Communication and Power

Burton (1990, p. 71) argues that 'our thinking is based upon an acceptance of the present as being the product of inevitable evolutionary forces.' Such inevitable evolutionary forces often find explanation and justification in history. These forces manifest themselves in an important triad: history, communication and power. Individuals or groups in conflict will be enmeshed in this triangular nexus as a conflict unfolds. History is defined as a perceived version of the past; it is an explanation of how things were, and why things today are as they are. It should be noted that all histories are value laden, and biased towards those who write them. The value-laden nature of history also points to another facet: not all history is factual. Histories often contain invented, reinterpreted or plainly fictional parts. Even the most 'factually' accurate history is filled with supposition, guesswork and fiction. Yet most of our focus here is not on the professional writer of history, but rather on the histories that all people possess. Not all histories are formally written; many are simply shared verbally. Although written histories may be found for nation-states, ethnic groups, religious sects, political parties, organizations, businesses and so on, there are countless other groups which do not possess such formal historical records. A group of employees in an office often do not share a written history of their past, yet they do have an oral history, one usually kept informally. Duryea and Potts (1993, p. 388) write:

> Every family, every society and cultural group, Native and non-Native, has its own stories. Some are based on historical incidents, some are pure myth. Each carries a message. Stories and myth are part of the 'glue' that holds a group of people together and helps provide its unique identity.

Myth and story are more often than not conflated in conflict resolution. Myth informs the format of the story, influences the values held, and their expression. The story is the history of a given event, person or place. Each group, Duryea and Potts (1993) note, has its story, which serves to explain and guide its actions, and serves to provide the conflict analyst with an important insight into the conflict.

Histories, either formal or informal, are communicated to group members. The process of communication has two end-products. One is the maintenance of ties between members of the group. In this sense, history becomes a regulator of individual behaviour, within the context of the group as a whole. Thus for group members to be group members they must accept the history of the group; that is, the version of realities gone by and their connection to the present must be accepted by group members. In this sense, a history is an ideological force. A second end-product of the communication of history is control. In the first instance, history regulated behaviour, created links between people. In the second instance history acts as a rather blunt instrument to keep group members in line, and acts as a boundary between a given group and non-group status.

Since histories are communicated and create boundaries between people, as well as providing values for individuals to follow, they can be said to be powerful. Power is exercised through the communication of history, in that by communicating history values can be allocated to individuals. A person's position *vis-à-vis* the history of the group may determine his or her ability to gain resources and may even influence that person's life chances.

An excellent example of the history–communication–power triad can be found in US race relations. African American social position is governed in large part by history. The history of social and economic relations, as it is currently articulated, governs the distribution of social resources. Communication of alternative histories had been considered dubious until the rise of African American studies programmes at universities, and even then alternative histories have had a difficult time obtaining any sense of broad legitimacy. The difficulty these alternative histories have had in gaining a foothold with wide acceptance reflects one of the very fundamental truths in deep-rooted conflict: histories are not easily changed. Northern Ireland, the Middle East, Bosnia, or elsewhere, all these places possess histories which explain and justify the conflicts. As Pruitt and Rubin (1986, p. 119) argue, 'Norms of all types, including those that encourage aggressive behavior toward the outgroup, tend to be self-perpetuating and hence often outlive the reasonable purpose for which they were first developed.' The norms to which Pruitt and Rubin refer are ensconced in the histories of groups. They outlive any usefulness they may have once had, because the perpetuation of a history is directly linked to power. Once power is won by way of a particular history, parties which support that given history would be loath to let it go.

The possible payoffs from being able to alter history are high, so much so that to alter history takes considerable effort. Therefore, to examine these payoffs and some of the difficulties encountered in trying to alter history, the connection between history and propaganda will be considered next.

History and Propaganda

The most effective way to classify the world, to separate one group from another, is to explain that classification in terms of history. The use of history is quite clear: it explains who we are and where we are going. Take, for example, the biblical book of Genesis, which explains human origins, the creation of biological sex, the origin of gender, and the separation of humans from animals. History is perhaps the most potent aspect of human communication in the conduct of conflict.

History can change, make no mistake about it. It is not the objective recounting of events. The past changes because it is written in the present. We select, embellish, create and invent history all the time. This is not to say that there is no element of truth in it, or that history is fiction. Rather, the 'facts' are interpreted, associated with other events and ideas. Different events receive more or less attention. All of this creates our past and our history.

Not all histories, of course, are written in books and published. In fact, few histories are written at all, or have the attention of historians. Most are recounted by the actors themselves, retelling an old story of past events and emphasizing the relevant parts for the audience. The person who recounts their divorce will tell a tale which explains why the event happened, they place blame where blame is due (in their eyes), and will carry within it the sense of justice or injustice signified by that event. The story is often retold in ritualized ways, emphasizing the same portions, using phraseology of a particular kind. History is also often used to explain why a given conflict cannot be resolved, why the parties are locked into an eternal fight.

From the perspective of social and structural conflict we are particularly interested in those histories which move groups. There are countless examples of groups involved in conflict who have an especially heightened sense of history. One would be hard pressed to find groups in conflict which did not have a strong sense of the past, but which were strongly motivated by the past. The group may be a neighbourhood watch committee, members of a local church, a union, an ethnic group, or even a nation. Any and all of these collectivities, when faced with conflict, will call up their histories to explain who they are and why they are in conflict.

It is important to note a difference between human groups and functional groups in how they encounter history. A human group refers to those collectivities, such as a nation, ethnic group or racial group, wherein membership is more often ascribed, and where the group absorbs the totality of the individual (as in impacting upon cultural forms such as eating habits, kinship systems, and beliefs). Functional groups are different from human groups, where membership is usually (though not always) assumed, and where membership does not absorb the totality of the individual. For example, Enloe (1986) argues that an ethnic group is a human group, where ethnicity 'informs a person where he belongs and whom he can trust'. An example of a functional group is found in a political party, where membership is voluntary, and can be easily changed. History plays a key role in both types of groups, but is of greater salience in human groups. One cannot easily imagine an ethnic group where history does not address the fundamental questions of personal identity and position.

An obvious example of a human group and the role of history in conflict can be found in nationalist movements. As Smith (1983, p. 22) argues,

> For nationalism may be described as the myth of the historical renovation. Rediscovering in the depths of the communal past a pristine state of true collective individuality, the nationalist strives to realise in strange and oppressive conditions the spirit and values of that distant Golden Age. The roots of the individual are buried in the history and ethos of his group, in its culture and institutions; and from these, and these alone, he can draw purpose and strength for the heroic deeds of the future.

Nationalist movements, or the simple nationalist drives found in patriotism, inform and motivate actors in conflict. Examples of strong nationalist movements include Zionism, the Afrikaners, German neo-Nazis and the Russian Black Shirts. Like culture, the nation acts to satisfy needs for the individual, and because it acts to satisfy needs, it is an important point of focus for conflict resolution. Ondrusek argues that such nationalisms can create truly difficult situations, and can be characterized by

> the tendency to find an enemy to blame instead of a pragmatic way to solve problems; the tendency to think within a totalitarian framework that makes a strong distinction between us and them; the tendency to assume that the other side has substantially different aims, values, and needs; and the use of propaganda to build informational walls that reinforce polarized, stereotypical thinking. (Ondrusek, 1993, pp. 246–7)

Such a polarized and rigid world does little to support liberal values and may quickly dissolve most attempts at resolution.

Afrikaner nationalism serves as an excellent illustration of the force of history in feeding, informing and influencing a conflict. Afrikaners, the descendants of Dutch and French Huguenot settlers in South Africa, have separated themselves from other collectives many times in the past. First, they separated themselves by leaving their home countries and settling in and around the Cape of Good Hope. Second, following the imposition of British rule in the Cape, Afrikaners left the Cape and moved inland, once again separating themselves. There followed a tradition of seeing the Afrikaner as somehow separate from and distinct from other groups of people. Around this idea there grew up a history to explain this distinctness. Leonard Thompson (1985, p. 46) comments:

> The Afrikaner nationalist mythology has been propagated through an elaborate network of religious, educational, and communications institutions. Not only has it dominated the historical consciousness of most Afrikaners, but it has also been imposed on the minds of other sections of the South African population.

The network for propagating the Afrikaner nationalist mythology has included such things as the mass media, print media and even the schools. Take, for example, education in Afrikaner schools:

> In school the teaching of history would revolve around the struggle of the Afrikaner. 'History is taught in such a way as to make the Afrikaner look good.' The Boer leaders were heroic figures who made immense sacrifices. They were depicted in a very sympathetic, uncritical light with stories of how the Boer families had trekked barefoot over the mountain tops and with photographs of women and children dying of hunger in the British concentration camps. European history was skimmed over – the French Revolution ... was dismissed as 'a mob that got angry'. The philosophical dimensions of the French Revolution and later European wars of liberation were barely touched on. (Leach, 1990, p. 71)

From the earliest age, Afrikaner children have been taught that they are different from, and separate from, the black African majority in South Africa. The process of classification once again shows itself. The extent to which this separateness is pursued is reflected even in the very definition of humanity. According to Thompson (1985, p. 29) some Afrikaners legitimated the former racial policies of South Africa by creating a

> mythology [which] presents the African inhabitants as a totally distinct subspecies of humanity. They are deemed to have arrived in South Africa no earlier than the first Dutch settlers and to have blindly resisted the spread of 'civilization,' which is regarded as an exclusively 'White' and 'Christian' achievement.

Growing out of this sense of history, then, was the Boer *laager*, or the Afrikaner wall behind which they 'protect themselves'. The history of Afrikanerdom was one in which there were always external threats, and the manner in which those threats were dealt with was to withdraw. Put in the context of human needs, the method through which Afrikaners sought to satisfy their needs was one of insulation and withdrawal. When needs satisfaction was threatened, the Afrikaners did exactly what one would have predicted: withdrew.

It is important to note, too, that the Afrikaner treatment of black Africans was also commensurate with their historical testament. Given the unique and even special divine status of the Afrikaner, as the bringer of Christianity to that part of Africa, the indigenous African was seen as something less than a human. To that end, of course, it would be impossible for the Afrikaner to trust the African, because the African did not follow God's law. Therefore, to allow the African to live in anything less than virtual captivity and total control was to invite disaster. Furthermore, how could one negotiate with the African, because, once again, the African was something less than human? Of course, events have demonstrated that negotiation can happen, perhaps signalling the demise of the Afrikaner nation.

For the nationalist Afrikaner, the history of the origins of the nation serves as a pervasive reminder of classification. The propaganda used to spread this nationalist message has been quite complex and sophisticated. Of course, not all groups use such sophisticated methods, nor does their history pervade all such activities as in the case of the Afrikaner. History has an especially powerful impact on the perceptions of the Afrikaner.

The Afrikaner sense of history has guided political decisions and behaviours. Decisions undertaken by Afrikaner leadership, as with any leadership, are guided by the exigencies of the day, as well as by historical influences. History also influences the ways in which we perceive the world around us.

History and Perception

The history that people possess not only influences the form that society takes, but also profoundly influences the perceptions they have of the world around them. Cohen (1992), for example, argued that when Christopher Columbus accidentally bumped into the New World his 'discoveries' were profoundly influenced by his intellectual and cultural preconceptions. When Columbus discovered people totally new to his experience he had to grapple to put them into context, a process which was influenced by his individual and collective past. When he encountered the people of what are now the Bahamian Islands he had five possible explanations of their identity, according to Cohen (1992). First, they could have been Asians whose appearance differed from what he was expecting; second, he had encountered some other group of known people; third, he had come across some as yet undiscovered group; fourth, he had discovered a group of unknown people who lived in an earthly paradise; and fifth, he had uncovered not humans, but near-humans who were in fact monsters. Columbus, apparently, opted to combine the fourth and fifth options; his perception was that the people of the New World had some monstrous practices, including cannibalism, yet were at the same time somehow denizens of paradise. That Columbus could have come to such conclusions is best explained by the conditioning that history had placed on him.

The labels that we attach to events in the world around us, particularly those events which have either no obvious explanation or an ambiguous explanation, are influenced by our history. If your history is guided by a belief that your people have been touched by the hand of God, then it seems likely that you will perceive yourself in a way very different from those who lack such special divine attention. The Branch Davidians, led by David Koresh, came to their end in Waco, Texas, by committing mass suicide, and the Jews who perished at Massada roughly two thousand years earlier both perceived the value of their lives very differently from others. Both groups boasted a special relationship with God, and because of the relationship both willingly ended their lives for the promise of something better.

History and Decision-making

History is not always tied to nationalism as such, or to one's relationship with a deity. It may instead be used by groups to define themselves, identify an enemy, and be a guide for action and decision making. During October 1962 the USA became embroiled in what has been called the Cuban missile crisis. The Soviet Union covertly based nuclear-tipped missiles in Cuba. The Kennedy administration reacted with considerable caution and purpose, and sought the removal of those missiles. After a brief period of stand-off, the missiles were removed from Cuba in an exchange for a promise by the USA not to invade Cuba. At first glance it does not appear that history had played much of a role in this event at all, yet that is far from the case.

Mazarr (1988) pointed out that US relations with Cuba have been guided by history for some time. Since the first half of the nineteenth century there has been in the USA a body of opinion that holds that Cuba is a natural part of the USA. Therefore, actions in Cuba were intimately tied to the USA. Indeed, following the seizure of Cuba from Spanish control following the Spanish–American War it appeared as if Cuba's destiny was sealed. Cuba was, however, given its independence, though that independence was guided by close economic and political ties to the USA. So, from the standpoint of the USA there have been historical 'justifications' and motivations that have informed US relations with Cuba, and these influenced US activity during the Cuban missile crisis. What acted as a stronger historical influence, though, was the US experience during the Bay of Pigs fiasco.

The Bay of Pigs was an operation originally planned by the Central Intelligence Agency, under the direction of the Eisenhower administration, but modified and carried out by the newly elected Kennedy regime. The operation was to consist of the training, equipping and delivery back into Cuba of Cuban exiles by covert means conducted by the CIA. The mission, however, ended in failure when the Cuban exiles were trapped on the beach by Cuban military forces, and when there was found to be insufficient air cover provided by the Cuban exile forces. President Kennedy declined to offer the exiles any further support once they landed on the beach, and there they foundered, and were overrun by the Cuban military. As a result of this operation, the USA and the Kennedy administration received a thorough condemnation throughout many parts of the world. The White House staff knew themselves that they had failed to conduct the operations with sufficient skill. As a result of the failure at the Bay of Pigs, the Kennedy administration established a commission of inquiry to ascertain the causes of that failure. According to Janis (1982, p. 140),

> Then, acting partly on his advisers' recommendations and partly on his own hunches, Kennedy introduced a series of sweeping changes in the decision-making procedures of his team to ensure that there would never again be a fiasco like the Bay of Pigs.

Against this backdrop of the failure of the Bay of Pigs operation the Kennedy administration sought to conduct itself differently during the missile crisis. Using explicit historical examples of what not to do, and what to say, they sought to conduct US foreign policy in the light of historical lessons. So explicit was their attention to history that Kennedy, after having read Barbara Tuchman's *The Guns of August*, remarked, 'I am not going to follow a course which will allow anyone to write a comparable book about this time, *The Missiles of October*' (Neustadt and May, 1986, p. 15). With this comparison in mind the Kennedy White House explicitly sought to avoid a repeat of the Bay of Pigs fiasco, as well as the opening of World War III. Kennedy undertook to alter the communication dynamics of the group, including de-emphasis of his role as leader, the encouraging of criticism, and the questioning of assumptions. He also sought to question the actions of the 'enemy', the USSR. Rather than simply assume that what the Soviets did was motivated by their enemy status, he sought to understand their actions. Instead of relying upon the propagated images that often informed action, the Kennedy administration sought new interpretations of Soviet action. They decoupled, if only for a moment, the link between history and propaganda, and tried to find new ways of linking the two.

There are, obviously, differences between the ways in which histories are used. In the case of Afrikaner nationalism, history serves to create boundaries through which intruders may not pass. These boundaries serve to delineate the group from the non-group. In the Cuban missile crisis example, history served as a guide and an explanation for action. Both cases serve to illustrate how history may be used in a conflict setting. History may itself create a sense of conflict, as in the Afrikaner example, where children are taught that the Afrikaner is alone and under threat. Or history may serve as a guide for how to conduct conflict, as in the Cuban missile crisis.

History and Human Needs

It will be useful to examine briefly how, or whether, history links with Burton's theory of human needs. While history has been recognized as playing a central role in the conduct of conflict and conflict resolution, it has yet to be placed within the context of conflict resolution theory. Most conflict resolution theory is ahistorical. History plays little or no role in the conduct of conflict resolution; at least, this is the impression one gets from the literature. Yet the connection between communication, history and human needs is clear. Communication acts as the vehicle through which social interaction, social control and social change occur. Interaction, control and change do not occur in a vacuum, however. Their occurrence is within a historical context, explicitly drawn on by social actors for information, guidance and justification. What is contained within that history is the record of how human needs are satisfied by that group. The socially legitimate and illegitimate methods for satisfying human needs are reflected in the history espoused by groups.

From a societal level, human needs satisfaction takes on a conservative note. Burton (1988, p. 19) comments, 'leadership and elites seek to conserve existing roles and institutions by whatever power means are at their disposal until overcome by more powerful forces'. History serves as the guide for the leadership and elites, as both explanation for and a model of needs satisfaction. Isaacs (1989, p. 118) believes that 'a principal function of the past is to legitimize the present'. For some, the present, with its roles and positions, offers a convenient pathway for needs satisfaction. Thus history provides the rationale that explains current needs satisfaction. Parties may even use explicit forms of propaganda in order to ensure and maintain the needs satisfaction process. The past becomes a persuader, and individuals and groups seek to defend the social institutions and roles that satisfy their needs.

Some human needs, as was pointed out earlier, are satisfied as if they were scarce. The need of identity, for example, may be distributed unevenly in a society. For example, Australian Aborigines were not permitted to be 'Australian' until 1967, when they obtained the right to vote. Historical explanations are used to justify the 'scarcity of identity', for example arguing that a certain group of people are too 'primitive' to be permitted to have a shared sense of identity. Burton (1990, p. 71) asserts that there can be no doubt that 'that past controls our thinking' and that 'our thinking is based on an acceptance of the present as being the product of inevitable evolutionary forces'. Yet we need not, of course, blindly accept our present-day conditions as being 'givens'. Certainly this was not the case when the Aborigines obtained the vote; the past was not written in stone and could, in fact, be changed.

It would appear, from this brief discussion, that history and human needs satisfaction share a tight bond. Needs satisfaction does not operate on such an abstract level that it occurs outside a given context. Burton has argued that needs are not in scarce supply – that, for example, the satisfiers of the need for recognition are unlimited. What may be scarce are the *apparent* means for satisfaction, which are culturally and historically defined. History serves as an explanation, often a rationalization, as to why a group is in the condition in which it finds itself. In this way, history is a conservative force, seemingly preventing people from finding new avenues for needs satisfaction.

Those who wish to understand conflict and move towards resolution must have an understanding of how to uncover this historical layer to a conflict. It would appear unlikely that one can speak meaningfully about resolving conflict without having a grasp of the past.

Using History to Analyse Conflict

To turn now to the use of history in analysing conflict, it appears that history is not only a feature of conflict, but also a most powerful analytical tool. Without a good sense of history, no conflict can be understood in a way meaningful for resolution. The importance of history cannot be over-emphasized. As Tillett (1991, p. 15) argues, 'the history of each [party] is important in understanding the origins and the nature of the conflict, in identifying the nature of the conflict, and in preparing for resolution'. At its most basic, history may reflect what happened between conflicting parties. Yet history does far more than just that; it also helps reflect what is going on in the minds of the parties in conflict, what their motivations are, and how they perceive that a given conflict might end. History is more than a mere description of the past; it provides insight into the deeper layers of meaning. Volkan (1979, p. 34) notes:

> The difficulty with descriptive studies is, of course, their limitations in respect to any probing of the unconscious forces that determine – or strongly influence – behavior patterns. One basic problem with studies summarizing what was said or done on a conscious level is that they are likely to be interpreted by shapers of foreign policy according to 'common sense' rather than with the insights available to students of intrapsychic process. Of course, even when psychological background is given to people unsophisticated in psychodynamic formulation, they may fail to grasp its implications; *but they will at least know that matters are more complicated than they seem on the surface to be* [emphasis added].

Whether it is a descriptive study, or the telling of history by a participant in conflict, the third party must do more than simply account for detail. As Volkan argues, the analyst must cut beneath the surface of the recounted history and search for deeper motivations and insights. Whether the analyst employs a psycho-analytic approach, or uses a human needs analysis, the key is to cut beyond the descriptive detail and access the more deeply seated sources of motivation. This is as true for a manager trying to resolve an organizational conflict as it is for the diplomat bringing together two warring factions.

For the analyst to come, understanding history as an important insight into the dynamics of a given conflict is an important step. Pruitt and Rubin (1986) offer some useful insights into how history may be analysed. They suggest that before conflicts occur, those more deeply seated forces, such as human needs or values, must become articulated in terms of goals or standards, or what they term aspirations. Parties with high aspirations are more likely to be embroiled in conflict than those with low aspirations. There are five determinants of aspiration levels: past achievement, perceived power, rules and norms, comparison with others, and the formation of struggle groups.

Past achievement refers to what has been obtained previously, and is directly linked to the level of aspiration. As one achieves more, argue Pruitt and Rubin (1986), one holds increasingly higher aspirations. When, however, achievements have led one to have sufficiently high aspirations that no aspiration satisfiers exist, then conflict erupts as parties search for satisfiers. An example of the operation of past achievement leading to conflict can be found in post-World War I middle America, where black soldiers returned from service in Europe only to experience continued racial barriers. Shortly following the war a number of very intense and violent riots erupted in a number of large US cities. Black soldiers, having served in uniform and experienced the horrors of combat, as well as having successful military service, returned to find a world that had not changed. While their achievements rose dramatically overseas, the domestic sources of aspiration satisfaction simply did not exist. Thus the achievements won in military service during wartime created conditions wherein these very successes, along with domestic racism and structural inequality, led to conflicts.

Another source of increasing aspirations is *perceived power*. Parties may perceive themselves to be stronger, and therefore in a better position to coerce another party. As has been already noted, power is a much-contested and subjective social phenomenon. Given its relative inexactitude it is not surprising that parties inaccurately assess their own level of power. History, both personal and national, abounds with examples of perceived power impacting upon levels of aspiration. At the turn of the last century, Cecil Rhodes and the economic interests he represented believed their power far greater than that of the Afrikaners. Rhodes and his cohorts launched Jameson's Raid in an effort to topple the Afrikaner government of Paul Kruger in the Transvaal. Much to Rhodes's surprise, however, the power of his interests in the Transvaal was much less than he supposed. Another example often mentioned is the overstatement of US power in Vietnam, where US policymakers believed their political power to be far greater than it actually was.

A third determinant of aspirations is in *rules and norms*. Rules and norms, according to Pruitt and Rubin (1986), determine the kind and level of things to which one can reasonably aspire. In British society not everybody can aspire to become king or queen, and therefore few try, whereas there are far greater numbers of British citizens who seek to become prime minister, though there again norms and rules of society curtail who can aspire to such a role. According to Pruitt and Rubin (ibid., p. 16), conflict will erupt when 'rightful aspirations seem incompatible with another party's apparent goals'.

A *comparison with others* is the fourth determinant of aspiration identified by Pruitt and Rubin (1986). Parties in physical or ideological close proximity with others will make comparisons between the two parties. As other parties are seen to be better off in some way, then that less well off party will seek to better itself. This kind of phenomenon is often seen in neighbourhoods where home-owners vie for having 'the best' house. Lawns and gardens grow and change in an unending cycle of 'keeping up with the Joneses'. As these comparisons are made, conflict may eventuate when one party sees itself unable to obtain, or unduly kept from obtaining, its aspired-to level. This kind of comparison is at the heart of class conflict.

The fifth and final determinant of aspirations is the *formation of struggle groups*. Pruitt and Rubin (1986, p. 16) write:

> When several people with similar latent (unrecognized) interests begin to talk with one another, their interests often rise into consciousness. Gaining the courage of their convictions, they may begin to develop and pursue new aspirations, which can lead to conflict with others whose interests are opposed to these aspirations. Such a result is particularly likely if they begin to identify themselves as a group apart from other groups. The common aspirations then become group norms, and the pursuit of these aspirations becomes a manifestation of group loyalty. The result can be called a struggle group.

Struggle groups are commonly found today in Western society addressing such subjects as environment, violence, race and taxes. These groups may be found in conflict either when they oppose a powerful group, or when their aspirations lead them to call for radical or even revolutionary change – in which case the defenders of the status quo will not long sit still.

These five determinants of aspiration are important for the study of conflict in that they provide historical focus. It is important to observe that each of the five determinants is tied to some sense of the past. The achievements of the past need not necessarily be linked to any recent past, but can be tied to the distant past instead. For example, in some conceptions of Israeli nationalism, there have been calls for the re-establishment of the kingdom of David, and the establishment of a historical Israel whose borders are based upon the achievements of past and long-dead leaders. Understanding the currents within Israeli history is a vital starting-point for understanding the dynamics of the current Middle East conflict. Equally, the analyst of conflict does not look for an 'objective' version of past achievements, but rather the version of past achievements which guides and motivates the actions of parties.

In the case of perceived power the analyst must ask how parties have come to see their own power the way that they do. What is the story that describes and explains the current perception of power, both in an absolute sense and in relation to others' power levels? Rules and norms also possess a history of how they came about, or over what they achieve. In comparisons with others there is a history of how the parties related through time. Is the comparison new, or is it a comparison that has existed over time? Many Canadians will compare themselves to Americans, describing in detail how Canadians and Americans are different. Is this comparison new, or does it have a much older history? If it is new, why is it new? If it is old, has it changed at all? Finally, the formation of struggle groups will have strong histories, from the perspective of both the group and those who oppose the group. Struggle groups will have detailed stories of how their attempts to organize have been opposed and undercut by those who oppose them. Their opponents will have histories that will vilify and clearly label the struggle group as being somehow deviant.

In each instance, the analyst must ask how the history reflects the inner state and types of behaviour exhibited by the parties. Not only does the history provide the analyst with some explanation of behaviour, but it also tells him or her much about the internal state of the parties. The process of recounting a history can tell much in terms of the level of emotional commitment and flexibility exhibited by the parties.

Conclusion: History, Conflict and Resolution

At heart, no conflict is possible without at least two contending histories. History, or the past, forms the basis from which all avenues of behaviour follow. A couple in the midst of a family conflict will call upon differing views and memories of the past, attempting both to explain and to justify their own behaviour, while at the same time vilifying the behaviour of the other. Groups do much the same with history, yet there is an added dimension. The communication of history acts as an important tool in maintaining group bonds, boundaries and objectives.

It is noteworthy just how often one can hear the refrain, 'let's forget the past' in an attempt to end conflict. This simple statement, usually offered as a commonsense approach to resolution, highlights the very importance of the past. The past has very real consequences for the present and future. Those who wish to quickly disarm an opponent will seek the seemingly simple ploy of decoupling the present and future from the past, but life and conflict are not that easy. Parties with much to lose or in power will often seek to decouple the past and present. Of course, the opposite is also true: weak parties will cling to their sense of history much more tightly than those with relatively more power. In this way it should be clear that history is a powerful and valuable resource in the conduct of conflict. It is also a strong force to grapple with in attempting to resolve conflict. The conflict in Northern Ireland is made more tenacious by virtue of the history of all sides to the conflict. These pasts cannot be erased, nor can they be easily wiped away. Montville (1992, p. 112) argues that

> healing and reconciliation in violent ethnic and religious conflicts depend on a process of transactional contrition and forgiveness between aggressors and victims. ... This process depends on joint analysis of the history of the conflict, recognition of injustices and resulting historic wounds.

Montville may be overstating matters, however. What may be more relevant is that parties acknowledge history, rather than seek any transactional contrition. Ultimately, while political leaders, like the

British prime minister, Irish prime minister, and even leaders of the major political parties in Northern Ireland, may make plans to resolve conflict, the psychological power and prowess of the historical roots of the conflict go untouched.

History plays a central role in the resolution of conflict. Most models of mediation have as one of the first steps that the parties in conflict describe the story, or the past, of the conflict. This is a clear recognition that one cannot plan for a resolution today without taking into account what has transpired in the past. This process of detailing the history of a given conflict serves several important purposes. First, it offers an opportunity to learn about the conflict from all sides. Second, it illustrates how the various parties perceive the conflict; it will highlight the similarities and the differences. Third, it will underscore the level of emotional commitment that parties have to the conflict. In describing a seminar where representatives from Northern Ireland discussed the history of the conflict, Montville (1992, p. 116) explained, 'The visitors left with a sense of new insight and common destiny which they said they had never experienced before.' So, while the articulation of history provides an opportunity to learn more of the factual detail of a given conflict, it also provides an opportunity to discover more about the emotional detail and commitments possessed by the parties. Without attention to history any conflict resolution process is bound to fail.

References

Blake, Robert R. and Jane Srygley Mouton (1984) *Solving Costly Organizational Conflicts*. San Francisco: Jossey-Bass.

Burton, John (1988) *Resolving Deep-Rooted Conflict*. Lanham, MD: University Press of America.

Burton, John (1990) *Conflict: Resolution and Prevention*. New York: St Martin's Press.

Cohen, I. Bernard (1992) 'What Columbus "Saw" in 1492', *Scientific American*, December, 56–62.

Duryea, Michelle LeBaron and Jim Potts (1993) 'Story and Legend: Powerful Tools for Conflict Resolution', *Mediation Quarterly* 10(4), 387–95.

Enloe, Cynthia (1986) *Ethnic Conflict and Political Development*. Lanham, MD: University Press of America.

Isaacs, Harold (1989) *Idols of the Tribe*. Cambridge, MA: Harvard University Press.

Janis, Irving (1982) *Groupthink*. Boston: Houghton Mifflin.

Leach, Graham (1990) *The Afrikaners*. London: Mandarin.

Maratsos, Michael (1979) 'New Models in Linguistics and Language Acquisition', in Morris Halle, Joan Bresnan and George A. Miller (eds) *Linguistic Theory and Psychological Reality*. Cambridge, MA: MIT Press.

Mazarr, Michael J. (1988) *Semper Fidel: America and Cuba 1776–1988*. Baltimore: The Nautical and Aviation Publishing Company of America.

Montville, Joseph V. (1992) 'The Healing Function in Political Conflict Resolution', in Dennis Sandole and Hugo van der Merwe (eds), *Conflict Resolution: Theory and Practice*. Manchester: Manchester University Press.

Neustadt, Richard E. and Ernest R. May (1986) *Thinking in Time*. New York: The Free Press.

Ondrusek, Dusan (1993) 'The Mediator's Role in National Conflicts in Post-Communist Central Europe', *Mediation Quarterly* 10(3), 246–7.

Pruitt, Dean and Jeffrey Rubin (1986) *Social Conflict*. New York: McGraw-Hill.

Simon, Herbert A. (1986) 'Alternative Visions of Rationality', in Hal R. Arkes and Kenneth R. Hammond (eds), *Judgment and Decision Making*. Cambridge: Cambridge University Press.

Smith, Anthony (1983) *Theories of Nationalism*. London: Duckworth.

Thompson, Leonard (1985) *The Political Mythology of Apartheid*. New Haven, CT: Yale University Press.

Tillett, Greg (1992) *Resolving Conflict: A Practical Approach*. Sydney: Sydney University Press.

Volkan, Vamik (1979) *Cyprus: War and Adaptation*. Charlottesville: University of Virginia Press.

7
ENEMIES

Introduction: Why Study Enemies?

The study of enemies provides an important link between the internal state, drives and motivations of the individual and society at large. The histories of conflict are replete with enemies. Our language is filled with terms that vilify and dehumanize enemies. Terms like 'scabs', for example, transform individuals into something less than human. Regardless of the conflict, be it international or interpersonal, the creation of an enemy is a central conflict process. It is a necessary dynamic in the evolution and continuation of a conflict, almost as if the process of creating enemies, or enmification, injects emotional power into a conflict. The study of enmification, within conflict resolution, has been relatively limited, however.

It should be noted that the study of creation of an enemy is different from the study of the opponent. All two- or multi-party conflicts have opponents; that is, at least one party against which an actor engages in conflict. An opponent is very different from an enemy, in that an opponent is not a value-laden being, such as Pol Pot. Rather, an opponent is simply an actor making choices, against which another party makes choices in an effort to gain their particular desired outcome. Extensive studies of 'the opponent' have been carried out in game theory, for example, where the behaviour of the opponent has been calculated as a series of rational choices.

The Importance of the Enemy

Some writers, such as Barash (1994), Coser (1968) and less so Simmel (1955), place a premium on enmity. Both Coser (1968) and Simmel (1955) argue that groups may benefit from the existence of enemies, inasmuch as enemies provide something around which group members may rally. This is perhaps best illustrated by political events in both the UK and the USA during World War II. In fighting the Nazis in the early 1940s both nations experienced a relatively high degree of cohesion. Opposition to the Nazis acted to bring together parts of society that in other times might not have cooperated.

Barash goes even further in exploring the value of enemies, arguing that

> enemies make history, not in the simple sense of producing important and noteworthy events, but in the deeper, literal sense of creating history itself. Without enmity, life – or at least, its political aspect – is deprived of meaning and literally seems to stop. (Barash, 1994, p. 10)

By way of metaphor, enmity is the fuel that drives human social behaviour and experience. Yet enmity is also a dangerous and destructive force and is responsible for many human tragedies.

An enemy is, in some way, an opponent, but also much more. An enemy is a value-laden, emotionally charged entity, one that is the recipient of specific negative value connotations and meanings. Enmification is the process of creating negative value associations with an opponent. These negative value associations may have many sources, some of which will be discussed below. Regardless of the source of enmity, however, it manifests itself in dividing the world up between 'them' and 'us'. The distinction between them and us leads to some important conflict dynamics. Pettigrew (1979) argues that poor behaviour on the part of *them* is attributed to their character and personality, whereas the same behaviour engaged in by *us* is excused and explained by situational factors. For example, management might believe that lies told by union negotiators are abhorrent, yet when management tell lies they are excused or justified by the demands of the situation. This process of excusing our allies, but damning our opponents, is known as the *ultimate attribution error*, and serves as a telling reflection of the way in which those in conflict see the world. Enmity is a subjective phenomenon, living in the minds of those who practise it. Keen (1991, p. 10) aptly comments, 'In the beginning we create the enemy. Before the weapon comes the image. We think others to death and then invent the battle-axe or the ballistic missiles with which to actually kill them.' People forgive their own trespasses more readily than they forgive those who trespass against them. Not only do people forgive themselves, but also through the process of enmification engage in acts of incredible cruelty.

Consider the Holocaust, in which some six million European Jews were killed by German forces. Goldhagen (1996) has created a startling account of the involvement of the average German citizenry in the brutality against the Jews. Goldhagen's thesis is in part that for such cruelty to be visited on the Jews it must have had support from the German citizenry. The source for such cruelty, says Goldhagen, was to be found in German anti-Semitism. He argues that this anti-Semitism was not simply some popular propaganda, but rather deeply seated within the German moral order and psyche:

> The underlying need to think ill of Jews, to hate them, to derive meaning from this emotional stance, woven into the fabric of Christianity itself, together with the derivative notion that Jews stand in opposition to the Christian defined moral order, create a readiness, an openness, if not a disposition, to believe that the Jews are capable of all heinous acts. All charges against the Jews become plausible. (ibid., p. 42)

The process of enmification in Nazi Germany began long before Hitler's rise to power. Equally, the origins of enmity in other social settings or contexts may also be as deeply seated as in Goldhagen's example.

The question arises, however, are people prisoners of their own nature, unable to do otherwise and locked into enmity? Or is it possible that humans can change, and escape the ultimate attribution error and the cruelty of enmity? This leads to a central question: can people escape enmity, or are they forever destined to have enemies?

Enemies by Nature?

A reasonable place to begin is to ask whether having an enemy is a healthy and normal human condition, or whether it is pathological. Coser argues that rather than look at the existence of an enemy as being pathological, it is best simply to understand the conditions under which enemies arise. He argues that some groups sought to create intragroup enemies, against which a struggle was launched. Coser (1968, p. 105) states:

> Just as [non-realistic or symbolic] ... conflict is governed not by the desire to obtain results, but by a need to release tension in order to maintain the structure of the personality, so the group's search for enemies is aimed not at obtaining results for its members, but merely at maintaining its own structure as a going concern.

This struggle against an enemy justified the existence of a group regime that would otherwise fall. Once the enemy was ousted, though, the group leadership faced a dilemma: they could either proceed with normal group business and face their own decline, or they could invent a new enemy. The words of W.I. Thomas, 'if men define their situations as real, they are real in their consequences' (quoted in Coser, 1968), are most apt when discussing the concept of enemy. Whether somebody or some group has actually done something or not to earn the mantle of enemy is immaterial. What is relevant is whether somebody *believes* them to be enemies. Shernock (1984, p. 302) argues that having an enemy becomes a method for survival for the group, and the conflict which creates the enemy is a 'means of sustaining a *legitimacy* for the continuity of group structure'. Enmity has been used, employing Coser's argument, for example, in the southern USA. African Americans have been enmified, cast in the role of enemy, in order to prop up social organization in favour of the whites. As Woodward (1974, p. 6) argues, 'The determination of the Negro's "place" took shape gradually under the influence of economic and political conflicts among divided white people — conflicts that were eventually resolved in part at the expense of the Negro.' The enmification of the African American serves as an example of the deeply seated nature of enmification. Enmification has also, of course, taken place elsewhere. There are countless other historical examples. Shernock (1984), for instance, argues that the Stalin show trials and the internal oppression by the Soviets was undertaken to justify and support the Stalinist regime. Finally, one cannot help wondering whether corporate inefficiency is not being established as a new enemy, justifying a corporate regime of job insecurity and restructuring.

Groups, and governments, may create internal states of emergency, resulting in conflict and the creation of enemies, to justify their own rule. This certainly seems to have been the case in South Africa under the leadership of P.W. Botha. The regime instituted an internal state of emergency in 1984, increasing state powers against what was seen as being a rising tide of politically motivated violence. Members of the African National Congress, Pan African Congress and other groups were cast in the guise of enemy. Also, while many anti-apartheid activists were enmified, the growing division within the white community demanded the creation of a new enemy, in order to maintain solidarity within the white ranks. Against this backdrop the state carried out forced removals of

shantytowns, and heightened its campaign against political opponents. The question still remains, though, whether this is a
pathological state, or whether it is simply the nature of all coercive
politics.

Others, though, hold the creation of enemies to be something
quite pathological. Spillman and Spillman (1991) describe the creation
of enemies as being a syndrome, and argue that 'Images of the
enemy are thus formed by a perception determined solely by
negative assessment' (p. 58). But if enmity is seen as a 'syndrome',
presumably it can be repaired. Evidently, too, it is a syndrome that is
encountered by whole societies. Holt and Silverstein (1989) assert
that repairing enemy images, or reducing the overly negative
perception of the syndrome, can be conducted through the process
of holding workshops and other consciousness-raising activities,
though with only limited success.

An important distinction should be made, it appears, between the
normal creation of enemies and the pathological state. The origins of
the creation of enemies also echo the distinction between the inherency
and contingency school. If one is to accept that enmity is the natural
by-product of the operation of our psyche, then perhaps the best we
can hope for is an assurance that it will not become abnormal. Or, on
the other hand, it may be that enmity is an entirely pathological
condition, in which case there is greater hope for a cure, provided the
illness is not rampant.

Enemies and the Archaic Past

There are those who see enmity as being as basic to humanity as
gathering food. The idea that there is an archaic past to enmity is
supported by archaeological discoveries of arrowheads and spear
points. It is interesting to speculate on whether the stone knife, bow
and arrows, or copper axe carried by the iceman found in the Italian
Alps were used for pacific or violent purposes. While the tools may
have been used for hunting, one cannot say for sure what was being
hunted – was it a woolly mammoth or somebody's cousin? Historian
John Keegan (1993, p. 3) writes, 'Warfare is almost as old as man
himself, and reaches into the most secret places of the human heart,
places where self dissolves rational purpose, where pride reins, where
emotion is paramount, where instinct is king.' He reminds us of the
Neanderthal pelvis bearing the remains of a spear wound, which by
itself may not be an indication of enmity, but it is surely suggestive
(ibid.). Should warfare be so ancient and as primordial as Keegan

would have us believe, can ancient enmity be far behind? How deeply seated is enmification?

Of course, the most deeply seated source of enmity would be found in our biological selves. Spillman and Spillman (1991) argue that there is a biological basis for enmification. They state that 'in escalating conflicts – be they among individuals or groups – the capacity of feeling one's way into the other (perspective-taking) disintegrates' (p. 62). The ultimate destination of this regression is early childhood. At this stage the world becomes one filled with simple dichotomies such as good/evil, us/them and strange/familiar. This early stage is a developmental stage that corresponds to the most ancient portion of the brain. The brain, for example, is divided into different levels, which correspond to the developmental evolutionary stages (Sagan, 1978). The neo-cortex, or outermost portion of the brain, is also the newest in evolutionary terms. The most ancient portion of the brain is the brainstem. Different portions of the brain govern different behaviours. Under normal circumstances our neo-cortex operates, giving us the ability to reason. Under stress, however, we regress, using more ancient parts of our brain.

Whether under stress or not, we divide the world into categories. Often, so Spillman and Spillman (1991) argue, these categories are stereotypes. They do not operate in a negative fashion, but simply assist us in making order in the world. Under the stress of escalating conflict, however, enemy images begin to arise. Spillman and Spillman (1991, p. 70) consider that these images 'are a pathological extreme of the functions of categorizing, distinguishing, and defining, that are so crucial to our survival, because they correspond to a regression to early childhood patterns of emotional functioning, perception and awareness'. Enemy images reduce or destroy the capacity to maintain perspective, and to see shades of goodness and badness.

Unlike Spillman and Spillman, Vamik Volkan (1990) feels that all humans have the need for enemies and allies. This need stems from the development of the child into an adult. Volkan's focus is on the development of ethnic identity and enemies. He argues that there are both good and bad self- and object-relations. Unmended self- and object-relations when externalized may in fact be healthy for the growing child. For example, they may be healthy for the self when externalized on an object of nationalist pride, such as a monument. They may be also be externalized, however, on to inappropriate 'objects' such as another ethnic group. As the self- and object-relations are externalized they build a psychic picture of the world, between the 'bad' recipients of this externalization and the good targets.

Volkan argues that the world of enmification is a complex and a sometimes contradictory world. In general, he sees two principles which guide enmification:

> the first deals paradoxically with ways in which we are like the enemy. There are often realistic reasons for enmity; in addition it is likely that we unconsciously perceive our enemy as a reservoir of our own unwanted parts and thus dimly acknowledge a fateful connection between us. We must not appear on the conscious level to resemble the enemy too closely, however, since it is necessary for us to believe that what we have externalized and projected upon him is not something of our own.
>
> The second principle, also paradoxical, concerns the distance maintained between a group and its enemy. On a conscious level we find ways to establish and control a distance from the enemy, while on an unconscious one our aggression toward the enemy binds us to him. Thus, both consciously and unconsciously, we become preoccupied with the enemy; in a sense, this makes for a closeness between us. (Volkan, 1986, pp. 176–7)

The enemy becomes the repository for our unwanted selves, yet as it is a repository we cannot let the enemy slip too far away, lest we lose control. Also, while we may wish to be far away from our enemies, we also find ourselves drawn to them, preoccupied with them. Lewin's concept of approach–avoidance conflict is applicable here. The conflict between wanting to approach an enemy and the drive to avoid the enemy at all costs is strong. Although approach–avoidance conflict, with relation to enemies, may often be intrapsychic, it may also become institutional, with political debates raging over just how to interact with an enemy. Such debates are found in labour–management relations, as well as in the USA over détente with the then USSR.

It is interesting to speculate on the purpose of enmity. Did the development of the enemy image arise from an evolutionary need? Enmity may have assured group solidarity, especially at times of scarcity. By creating the conditions wherein group members would, without thought, condemn members of a foreign or alien group, enmity may have been followed by an increase in the tenure of a given group on a piece of land or in social status. Yet as with so many arguments of this kind, it remains unclear whether enmity serves an evolutionary purpose. If it did serve an evolutionary purpose, the question arises concerning its continued functionalism. If no longer functional, can the process of creating enemy images ever be avoided or halted? It may be that enmity serves some function, or it may be that it is an offshoot of some other process. Of course, the creation of enemies may serve no purpose at all, there may be no function; it may simply happen.

Causes of Hatred and Alienation

Outlined above were several arguments relating to the archaic nature of enmity. There are other possible causes, which are many and varied. Perhaps the first cause is the most obvious: some parties are cast in the role of enemy because their desire is to do irreparable harm to another party. Thus their enemy status is not undeserved, though it might be morally repugnant. Even so, this does not explain why the exact behaviours associated with enmification occur. Still, it is worth remembering that some 'enemies' are so named because of very clear causes.

That aside, however, there are countless enemies who have not earned that label. To link Deutsch (1973, 1991) and Coser (1968), indices may be created that are useful in identifying situations where hatred and violence may erupt. These are the situations in which dehumanization and enmification may occur. First is an increase in relative deprivation, where war, drought and any other cause of increased economic dislocation leads to the identification of enemies. Obviously, one can find those responsible for war, or at least arguably responsible for war. Finding those responsible for drought, however, is another matter. Still, by using such ideas as 'impurity' or 'satanism', people can be blamed for natural disasters and be labelled enemies.

A second source of hatred and violence may stem from group instability, where leaders seek enemies to divert attention from their own problems. Leaders of unstable political regimes, be they leaders of states or smaller groups, may undertake to vilify some person or group in order to focus attention away from other issues.

Authoritarianism is a third condition leading to hatred. Rigid organizations often receive the enmity of their employees. Environments where people are proscribed from expressing themselves become hotbeds of enmity.

Claims of superiority, such as racial, ethnic and religious superiority, may be another source of hatred and enmification. The earlier example of Nazi Germany, with claims of Aryan superiority, serves as an obvious illustration of the impact of superiority on the process of enmification. Racial and ethnic superiority are particularly difficult areas with which to cope. Unlike other forms of enmification, ethnic and racial enmification occur (usually) in situations where individuals are in contact. In many other settings, such as international conflict, we do not come into direct contact with our 'enemies', and this has an impact on how we engage in conflict.

Hatred and enmification may occur when violence, structural or actual, is the norm. Enmification occurs in highly violent societies almost as a matter of course. When violence is a cultural value, it seems as if there must be some justification for its targets. One would presume that in societies where violence is a norm, enmification is equally to be expected.

Another source of enmity and hatred is found in situations where there is a lack of human contact, engagement and bonding. With few opportunities to meet, parties may find it easy to cast others in the role of enemy. Stories can be heard among Afrikaners who tell of travelling only in their immediate circle of friends, never interacting with any non-Afrikaners. In this situation, it is not surprising that some Afrikaners may have created enemies out of black Africans. After all, the black Africans were 'out there' and unknown to the whites. This story can be retold in many suburban parts of the USA, where white Americans rarely interact with African Americans, or, again, retold in Australia, where Australians of European descent rarely if ever interact with Aboriginal Australians.

The final area of focus concerns situations where there is no strong objection to hatred and enmification. Often such objections must come from outside the group or situation. Situations that lead to hatred and alienation may occur because there is no check on its occurrence. Without anyone to keep a watch, some people may simply go on a rampage of uncontrolled vilification.

Each of these situations may alone, or in combination, serve as the basis for enmification. This list, though, provides little reflection on sources of enmity that may be biological. If enmity is biological, then such a list is of little assistance in the prevention of enmification.

The search for the causes of enmity leads back to the question of inherency versus contingency. For example, enmification may have an evolutionary impulse, wherein it takes place to ensure that the positive aspects of aggression are experienced. Recall that Lorenz, for example, argued that there are positive reasons for aggression, such as ensuring that the population is distributed and not overcrowded. If this is the case, then it appears as if there is little capacity to prevent or interrupt the process of enmification. Or if we presume a more interactionist approach, then it may ·be that enmification occurs as a result of a variety of factors. For example, to draw on the work of Spillman and Spillman (1991), who argue that increasing levels of conflict are paralleled by regression into more basic neuropsychological states, it may be that some people are more able to withstand this regression. In other words, while there may be a biological explanation for enmification, it may be that enmification is also influenced by social factors, which impact on individuals differently.

Identity and the Enemy

Some people love to fight, or so it appears. *Battuo ergo sum*, or 'I fight, therefore I am', is the often implied or stated viewpoint of many. How is it that conflict becomes integrated into a person's very soul? Why do some people hold to conflict with a historical enemy so strongly?

While writing about ethnic identity and its impact on intractable conflicts, Northrup has provided a useful outline of how one may come to enmify. There are four key stages to the process, which are threat, distortion, rigidification and collusion. The key to the process is found in identity, which Azar, Burton and others argue to be one of the fundamental drives of human behaviour. Identity, argues Northrup (1989), is a dynamic force, however, and is not fixed. The beginning of enmity rests upon a threat to identity. *Threat* occurs when 'in the course of a relationship between parties, an event occurs that is perceived as invalidating the core sense of identity' (ibid., p. 68). Being invalidated, of course, the recipient feels threatened, and may in return seek to threaten others as a form of defence.

The second stage of the process is *distortion*, which is seen by Northrup as being a psychological response to threat. Distortion refers to events where meanings are forced on to threats, or situations that invalidate one's sense of identity, which do not match the event itself. In other words, distortion is simply the taking in of a message, and denying or altering its meaning in order to reduce the threat. Distortion is similar to the reduction of cognitive dissonance, inasmuch as a party may experience a message and may wish to find a way to reconcile that message with an existing belief system. Thus distortion is an attempt at adaptation and protection.

A third stage is *rigidification*, defined by Northrup (1989, p. 70) as 'a process of crystallization and hardening what is construed as self and not-self'. As distortion is aimed at protecting the self from unwanted attacks on identity, the process of rigidification is the process of building a wall of protection. Initially, threats are dealt with in a piecemeal fashion, each individually thrust aside. As they continue, however, a unified and coherent process emerges where the defences are ideologically integrated. Part of the process is a clear differentiation between 'us' and 'them', or, in Northrup's terms, self and not-self.

The final stage is *collusion*, where parties come to assist one another in the maintenance of the conflict. The rigidification of responses to threats takes on an identity-like characteristic; it becomes incorporated into the self. As this occurs, the original threat and conflict take on important self-defining characteristics. The conflict – its history and its objectives – becomes part of those engaged in it. Parties to the conflict, who now find identity needs satisfied by the conflict, collude, tacitly or otherwise, in its maintenance.

The four stages of threat, distortion, rigidification and collusion combine to create a powerful force in conflict. Threat challenges identity, which begets defence, which becomes integrated into identity. The end result is that the conflict becomes profoundly embedded into the very essence of those engaged in it. Attempts at resolution, then, certainly must cut far more deeply into the collective psyche of the feuding parties than may originally be anticipated. Maintaining one's focus on the issues of the conflict, as opposed to deeper causes, simply ensures the continuance of the conflict. Northrup has provided a useful explanation of how violent, intractable, deep-rooted conflict becomes so profoundly integrated into the identity of individuals.

Dehumanizing Your Friends

Part of Northrup's outline of the creation of enmity requires a thought trick. The party being threatened must be able to justify their own actions in defence of the threat. Rigidification, or the division of the world into two camps, requires that those who are not-self are something less than self. This requires the dehumanizing of the enemy, and suggests that dehumanization is the precursor to enmification. Keen (1991, p. 25) notes:

As a rule, human beings do not kill other human beings. Before we enter into warfare or genocide, we first dehumanize those we mean to 'eliminate.' Before the Japanese performed medical experiments on human guinea pigs in World War II, they named them *maruta* – logs of wood. The hostile imagination systematically destroys our natural tendency to identify with others of our species.

A first step to killing – especially that as reflected in the tsarist pogroms of the late 1800s, the Turkish genocide against the Armenians, the German destruction of the Jews, the American decimation of the native peoples, or the ethnic cleansing of Bosnia – is dehumanization. The end of many lifelong careers, a modern version of socio-economic homicide, occurred after the dehumanizing effects of corporate downsizing and human resource management. Barash (1994) considers the dehumanizing process, writing, 'Thus, we find words such as "rats", "dogs", "vermin", "scum" and "pigs" applied to "the enemy" not just in the English language but also in German, Arabic, Japanese, Russian, Hindi, and Swahili, among others' (p. 88). Dehumanization is an intense psychological process, where differences between ally and enemy are exaggerated. The process divorces people from guilt, and instead creates a web of rationalization, justifying and explaining enmity. Furthermore, a group will take perverse pleasure at the prospect of destroying the enemy, because this too will enable the group to maintain its identity, which is in part a negation of the enemy.

Thus the first step in the creation of an enemy is a symbolic one: it is the symbolic transformation of an individual or group from human to something other than human. One need only briefly reflect on the plethora of racial slurs to observe that they draw on a litany of non-human characters. It would be a mistake, however, to view dehumanization in absolute terms. There are degrees of dehumanization. In combat, enemies develop names for one another, usually implying that the enemy is less than human, though there are some apparent contradictions. In the US Civil War Southerners were known as 'Johnny Reb', in World War II the Germans were sometimes referred to as 'Jerry' and in the Vietnam War US soldiers referred to the enemy as 'Charlie'. In each case, the enemy was given a human name. Does this suggest that dehumanization is not, in fact, a feature of enmification?

The existence of such human names for the enemy could, in fact, indicate that such dehumanization does not always occur. I think this unlikely, however, especially when one considers the origins of the names listed above. In each case they are derisive and dehumanizing, and at the same time personal. Johnny Reb is simply a play on words, where Reb stands for rebel. As dehumanizing goes, this is a rather weak epithet, but that is not surprising. The American Civil War was characterized not by two clearly distinct ethnic groups fighting one another, but rather by two groups of rather similar people fighting over a clearly political cause. The very fact that family members did fight on either side of the war augurs against enmification. Dehumanizing one's brother might backfire, leading to one's own dehumanization. Calling an enemy Johnny Reb is a safe, mild form of dehumanization.

'Jerry', another name of a person, would suggest that this is another case of mild dehumanizing. The origin of jerry, however, is a five-gallon water can, the jerry can. This German product is hardly human, and, while it is far from being profoundly insulting, it nonetheless suggests that the American and British soldiers who used this term were distancing themselves from their enemies.

Finally, referring to the Vietnamese as 'Charlie' seems on the surface to be anything but dehumanizing. Yet Charlie stood for the letter 'C', which itself stood for communist. To call somebody Charlie was to refer to them as a communist. Once again, this is a dehumanization, inasmuch as it refers to somebody as being a thing, and not a person. The American nationalist ideology holds a communist in very low regard, as being a collectivized, atheist foreigner who wishes to destroy the American way of life and replace it with some version of hell on earth – or so the extreme version would go.

In each of these cases dehumanization occurred, not apparently to the depth that Keen indicated was happening in World War II Japan. Of course, in each of those three wars there were far more degrading and dehumanizing terms used to describe the Southerners, the Germans and the Vietnamese, just as in the example from Japan, there were those who used far less derisive terms for their prisoners. Yet the fact remains that many of the terms used in common practice suggest that there is variation in the level of dehumanization. One way to ascertain the level of dehumanization is to examine both the terms being employed, and the variation of terms. Which terms are used depends, in part, upon what terms are available and how those terms are employed within the enemy system.

The Enemy System

Enmity appears to outlive those who practise it. Like a family heirloom, it is often handed down from generation to generation. Within a generation, enmity often is passed around from person to person, with little inhibition to its transmission. The question remains, how does enmity leap from person to person? This appears to be especially difficult if one accepts Volkan's description of the evolution of the image of the enemy; Volkan's version of enmity is highly individual and personal. Mack (1990) has suggested that the link between the individual and collective enmity finds its beginnings in the development of the child. A child, argues Mack (ibid.), is powerless and in a search for empowerment attaches to those who are powerful. Of course, the most powerful person, at first, in the child's development is mother. As the child ages, other powerful actors appear: father, siblings, cousins, neighbours and so on.

Politicians and purveyors of nationalism, so Mack (1990) believes, vie with parents for the child's attention. Even at a very early age, children are recruited into the system of enmification. Political leadership mandates that children recite nationalistic slogans, encounter stories of heroic bravery undertaken in the name of the group, and re-enact them through playgroup encounters with would-be enemies. Mack's argument is not unfamiliar; it is one which regards the source of enmity as being located in how and what children are taught. American children who watch cartoons like *G.I. Joe* are indoctrinated into systems of enmity. Thus the enemy system is found to be a rather simple contest for attention. Those with the greatest power, who can gain access to the attention of an audience, will be able to manipulate them into prearranged versions of enmity.

This version of enmification helps inform the activities of such propagandists as Josef Goebbels, the Nazi Minister for Information and Propaganda. This is the Madison Avenue advertiser's view of enmity, which implicitly holds that within each of us is an untapped, or perhaps easily refocused, pool of hate. With the right advertising campaign, this enmity can be turned on whatever the powerful feel to be appropriate. There is, obviously, some truth in this view of humanity. There certainly have been times when enmity has been turned on like a tap of running water. Yet even when enmity is unconnected to deeper historical pools it usually does last. The Bush administration attempted to vilify Saddam Hussein with rhetoric that equated the Iraqi leader to Adolf Hitler. Few Americans were out in the street protesting against Saddam as a modern-day fascist. The difficulty in vilifying him was that there was no historical motivation for the person in the street to accept such vilification, at least not at such short notice. Most anti-Arab feeling in the USA is left over from the Arab–Israeli Six Day War, and has abated considerably over the years. Even though many, if not most, Americans fail to distinguish between Iraqis and Iranians, not even the pool of enmity towards Iran and a confused American psyche could attach much meaning to Saddam Hussein. The attempt to enmify Saddam Hussein failed because it was based upon a simplistic and flawed view of enmity in general.

Rather, the enemy system has some parts that Mack leaves untouched, such as historical tradition. Had the Bush administration sought to equate Saddam Hussein with the Ayatollah Khomeini it would have found a more vigorous response. The majority of Americans still flinch when the late Iranian leader is mentioned. Given that most Americans confuse the ethnic, linguistic and religious background of the Arabs and the Farsi-speaking Iranians, the Bush administration would have done well to cast the Iraqi leader as another Khomeini. Of course, that Bush did not make such a move might suggest that he was unwilling to do so, perhaps because of his unsureness over what the Iranian government was planning to do during the Gulf War. Bush, left looking for a villain with whom to compare Saddam, took up one from his generation – in fact, *the* villain from his generation – and used that image.

Systemic enmity has, however, a key role to play in the exercise of political power, as evidenced by the dictatorship of Josef Stalin. In many respects, Stalin operated the process of enmification through the simplistic methods characterized by Mack and others – namely that there was a body of enmity awaiting direction. The Moscow show trials of the 1930s, in which Stalin's regime tried enemies of the state, was the creation of political enmity in the extreme. Stalin did, however, recognize the need to have some historical basis for enmification, in that he often selected former opponents as leaders of fictional conspiracies. So, while not steeping enmification in the historical traditions of the Russian and new Soviet peoples, he did attempt to link enmity to some sense of the past.

Whether the examples are drawn from democratic states or those with a more totalitarian bent, the transmission of mass enmity for public consumption is a media event. Prior to the advent of the movies, radio, television and cable, transmission of enmity depended upon other, slower means. Today's digitized high-speed media can play a central role, accessing millions of audience members. The

Internet, with its relative ease of access, provides a new platform upon which enmity can be enacted. Winter, in two studies of the impact of the media on enemy images in the USA concludes that:

> On the basis of these two studies, the media appear to send the message 'Although we want friendship and peace, they want power, domination, and war.' In cognitive terms, the distortion displays the classic defence mechanisms of projection and rationalization in which the enemy's putative power orientation provides a justification for one's own reluctant but necessary retaliation (or preemption). Thus, the tendency of the media to enhance an enemy's power-motive imagery ... can be a powerful dynamic of escalation in many kinds of conflict situations. (Winter, 1987, p. 45)

The presentation of one side as reasonable, while the other is supposedly motivated only by the cruellest avarice, is not surprising. Thus the perpetuation of the enemy system, through the use of the media and propaganda, may rely upon simplistic dualisms of good and evil.

Although the heavy hand of the media in the creation of enemy images may be one possible source of enmification, it is surely not the only source. Jewish nationalism did not simply cast Jews as good and the Romans as evil, but rather wove a long and intricate web of detail which explained both the inherent goodness of the Jews and the obvious evil of the Romans. For the Jews, the enemy image of the Romans found sustenance in such tales as the enslavement in Egypt, the Babylonian captivity, and other stories. Enmity finds much of its basis in history, either in direct recounts of transgressions against a specific people by a specific people, or by analogy. Julius (1990, p. 100) defines historical enmity as 'the internal representation of past historical events with their attendant emotional after effects. It is the way in which we mentally capture and retain the perceived meaning of certain past interactions with others.' Historical enmity may also take on the characteristics of beliefs within a group. Such beliefs may serve as the foundation of racial and ethnic enmity, for example. It is often interesting to hear people speak of the historical conflict between Jew and Muslim. Yet this historical conflict is sometimes hard to unearth in the annals of history. There were times when Jew and Muslim fought side by side and shared no enmity at all. Like all remembrances of things past, it is often useful to ask who is doing the remembering, and just what past they are recalling.

Enemies are often inherited, along with ethnic identity, group membership and family heritage, to name a few. So, while the purveyors of instant enmity may abound, ready to issue any new propaganda proclamation, it is the deeply held historical enmity that is most problematic. This sort of enmity is what we find in Burton's concept of deep-rooted conflict, involving deep feelings, values and needs which are left unaffected by the actions of any outside party who simply seeks to nullify history. Historical enmity and deep-rooted conflict share the seemingly unending display of conflictual behaviour, including violence. One common way in which historical enmity is expressed is through the operation of ethnocentrism and xenophobia.

Ethnocentrism and Xenophobia

Ethnocentrism, or the belief in the primacy and centrality of one's own culture, may serve as a precursor to enmification. All cultures, without exception, contain within them the seeds of ethnocentrism. How ethnocentrism may shift from being a normal cultural behaviour and become the seeds of enmification is not clear. Enmification growing out of ethnocentrism may arise out of perceived stress and pressure. For example, as Iranian culture experienced the importation and development of new cultural forms under the most recent shah, there may have also been an increase in cultural stress. Cultural stress is defined as tension which is shared among members of a given cultural group, and which leads individuals to experience the feeling of 'displacement'. In Iran, individuals appear to have experienced a sense of cultural stress, and to have adopted strategies to cope. Among these coping strategies was the rise of religious fundamentalism, as well as the enmification of the West and more specifically the USA. The extent of the vilification of the USA is best reflected in the Iranian use of the phrase 'The Great Satan', referring to the USA. It is significant that a major enemy of Iran was outside the country. Harking back to Coser's work, this suggests that enmification could have been used to create internal cohesion and bonding between members of Iranian society.

Xenophobia, or the unfounded fear of other cultures, also serves as an important influence on the process of creating enemies. The fear of the other, whether originating in some developmental stage of the child, or somehow linked to the biological origins of the person, or being formed from the crucible of human interaction, serves to isolate one culture from another. Xenophobia is sometimes presented in the most peculiar way. The American late-night comedy show *Saturday Night Live* used to have a comedy sketch in which the actors dressed and portrayed themselves as killer bees. Killer, or Africanized, bees are a strain of bee bred and released into the wild in South America. The intention was to create a bee that produced a higher volume of honey. What the breeders got instead was a highly aggressive bee, with a tendency to swarm. The bees have been making a slow trek northwards towards the US–Mexican border. One *Saturday Night Live* sketch in particular had the comic bees speaking with what were arguably Mexican accents. Thus the killer bee from Latin America had become a northward-bound Mexican. Paralleling this story was the increase in the number of illegal aliens crossing from Mexico into the southwestern USA. One cannot help but see the linking of the killer bee to the Mexican as being a metaphor for the much-feared surge of Mexicans into the USA. Most xenophobia does not, however, take on comic overtones, but rather serves as the basis of everyday perpetuation of the enemy image. Increasing diversity throughout the industrialized world suggests that the effects of xenophobia will be felt for some time to come.

It should be pointed out, however, that all cultures seem to have some levels of xenophobia and ethnocentrism, though not all cultures appear to experience deep-rooted conflict. Therefore, there is something more in operation in deep-rooted conflict than simple xenophobia and ethnocentrism, and that something may turn out to be historical enmity.

Intragroup Enmity

Throughout this chapter the focus has tended to be on two distinct groups, with enmity forming within one group against another. This, however, is not always the case. Groups may come to enmify some of their own members, with the result often being that that member is ostracized from the group. There are countless examples of individuals who have broken group norms in such a way that rather than suffering some sort of group chastisement, they instead are banished. Banishment, however, is rarely conducted in a value-free context; it is often accompanied by ideological condemnation as well. Many of the same processes operate in the context of intragroup enmity as operate in intergroup enmity. For example, group leaders may still engage in a propaganda campaign against the offending group member, in order that a group ideology forms around the violation of group norms. Or if one accepts Northrup's thesis that

enmity may form around the threat to identity, then one might
expect the rigidification and dehumanization to grow more organ-
ically from a variety of different group members, with a range of
status and role.

Group enmity may also be aimed not just at one person, but at a
whole segment of the group. A precursor to this situation, where a
group will essentially split in two, is group polarization. There is
some interesting experimental evidence on the impact of discussion
on group attitudes. The expectation was that with discussion would
come greater tolerance and even a convergence into consensus. Yet
in a variety of experiments, as reported by Baron *et al.* (1992),
intolerance actually increased: extremists became more extreme.
What this suggests is that in any group there is an undercurrent of
dissensus which does not always become expressed. When
expressed, however, it may solidify into apparently ideological
positions. Dissensus may act as a threat to the ideological centre that
the group had previously formed. This process is reminiscent of
Northrup's rigidification, where opinion becomes rigid following a
threat to identity. The rigidification, however, is not against some
outside force, but rather against members of one's own group.

For example, it may be that a group of employees have never
talked about a whole variety of issues. Yet around their job there is
an appearance of uniformity, out of which has grown a set of group
norms. Upon discussion of issues, however, it may emerge that there
are threats to the group norms that were previously unknown. Thus
there emerges a new group, evolving out of polarization. This new
group may come to be enmified by the original group and even
exiled. Thus it would seem that enmification within a group is not an
unlikely occurrence.

Conclusion: Enmity and Conflict Resolution

Enmification is present in any conflict one wishes to consider. Why
humans engage in the creation of enemies remains uncertain,
though many have made their suggestions. What seems unlikely,
though, is that enmification is the sole source of conflict, or even
often a cause of conflict. It is certain that the creation of enemies is
a by-product of conflict, but whether it rests at the centre of conflict
is unclear. Burton, for example, has argued that conflict finds its
origins in far more deeply seated drives than simply the search for
enemies. From Burton's perspective, then, enmification follows the
eruption of conflict. Volkan, on the other hand, sees enmification at

the base of conflict, because enmification reflects the inner development of the human psyche.

There is always difficulty in discussing the creation of enemies. It is the old chicken-and-egg question: which came first, the drive to enmify or the conflict which demanded the process of enmification? If such a drive for enemies does in fact exist, then the Gulf War was a convenient, and predictable, event, both for the Iraqis, which had just finished their war with Iran, and for the West, which had emerged victorious from the Cold War. Both, in their own ways, were itching for an enemy, perhaps even suffering from some kind of withdrawal symptoms. While it appears that enmification is a common phenomenon, found in most, if not all, cultures, it remains to be seen whether it, by itself, is the cause of conflict. I believe that that is unlikely to be the case. Like Burton, I would argue that the causes of conflict are deeper than the drive for enemies. Yet even if enmification is not the cause of conflict, its process certainly prolongs and perpetuates conflict, standing in the way of effective resolution. Understanding the processes and types of enmification is central towards any kind of meaningful resolution of conflict. It is a sure bet that while one looks for the root causes of conflict, one must at the same time deal with the very real phenomenon of enmification.

References

Barash, David P. (1994) *Beloved Enemies*. New York: Prometheus Books.

Baron, Robert, Norbert Kerr and Robert Miller (1992) *Group Process, Group Decision, Group Action*. Milton Keynes: Open University Press.

Coser, Lewis A. (1968) *The Functions of Social Conflict*. London: Routledge and Kegan Paul.

Deutsch, Morton (1973) *The Resolution of Conflict*. New Haven, CT: Yale University Press.

Deutsch, Morton (1991) 'Subjective Features of Conflict Resolution', in Raimo Väyrynen (ed.), *New Directions in Conflict Theory*. London: Sage Publications.

Goldhagen, Daniel Jonah (1996) *Hitler's Willing Executioners*. London: Abacus Books.

Holt, Robert R. and Brett Silverstein (1989) 'On the Psychology of Enemy Images: Introduction and Overview', *Journal of Social Issues* 45(2), 1–11.

Julius, Demetrios A. (1990) 'The Genesis and Perpetuation of Aggression in International Conflicts', in Vamik Volkan, Demetrios Julius and Joseph Montville (eds), *The Psychodynamics of International Relationships*. Lexington, MA: Lexington Books.

Keegan, John (1993) *A History of Warfare*. New York: Alfred A. Knopf.

Keen, Sam (1991) *Faces of the Enemy*. San Francisco: Harper.

Mack, John E. (1990) 'The Enemy System', in Vamik Volkan, Demetrios A. Julius and Joseph V. Montville (eds), *The Psychodynamics of International Relationships*. Lexington, MA: Lexington Books.

Northrup, Terrell A. (1989) 'The Dynamic of Identity in Personal and Social Conflict', in Louis Kriesberg, Terrell A. Northrup and Stuart J. Thorson (eds), *Intractable Conflicts and Their Transformation*. Syracuse, NY: Syracuse University Press.

Pettigrew, T.F. (1979) 'The Ultimate Attribution Error: Explaining Allport's Cognitive Analysis of Prejudice', *Personality and Social Psychology Bulletin* 5, 461–76.

Sagan, Carl (1978) *The Dragons of Eden*. London: Hodder and Stoughton.

Shernock, Stanley Kent (1984) 'Continuous Violent Conflict as a System of Authority', *Sociological Inquiry* 54(3), 301–29.

Simmel, Georg (1955) *Conflict*. New York: The Free Press.

Spillman, Kurt R. and Kati Spillman (1991) 'On Enemy Images and Conflict Escalation', *International Social Science Journal* 43(1), 57–76.

Volkan, Vamik (1986) 'The Narcissism of Minor Differences in the Psychological Gap between Opposing Nations', *Psychoanalytic Inquiry* 6(2), 175–91.

Volkan, Vamik (1990) 'An Overview of Psychological Concepts Pertinent to Interethnic and/or International Relationships', in Vamik Volkan, Demetrios Julius and Joseph Montville (eds), *The Psychodynamics of International Relationships*. Lexington, MA: Lexington Books.

Winter, David G. (1987) 'Enhancement of an Enemy's Power Motivation as a Dynamic of Conflict Escalation', *Journal of Personality and Social Psychology* 52(1), 41–6.

Woodward, C. Vann (1974) *The Strange Career of Jim Crow*. New York: Oxford University Press.

8
A CRITIQUE OF
RESOLUTION PROCESSES

Introduction: The Process of Resolution

Up to this point the emphasis has been on the dynamics that impact upon conflict. We turn now to the process of conflict handling or, popularly, conflict resolution, which means examining the dynamics that influence conflict resolution processes. Resolution means many things to many people, and therein lies difficulty. To some, resolution simply means an end, and therefore conflict resolution means merely the end of conflict. Thus for some, resolution may include such things as victory in battle, an opponent simply vanishing, or other such conclusive events. For others, resolution means a very specific kind of an end to conflict, where the means and methods are prescribed to be non-violent, participatory and voluntary. In most conflict resolution literature it is the latter that has gained the greatest attention. The focus of this chapter will, ultimately, be on this latter variety, though both kinds of resolution will be canvassed, in order that their similarities and differences, and strengths and weaknesses may be appreciated.

A couple of examples of definitions of resolution are in order. It should be noted that whatever definition is employed will have an impact on the process that ensues. Heitler (1990, p. 6) notes that conflict resolution occurs 'only when both sides share a willingness to pursue mutually optimal solutions'. Such a resolution employs a process that is also characterized by talk and largely cooperative behaviour. Heitler's approach to resolution is a therapeutic one, and her target audience consists mostly of those encountering interpersonal conflict. This, however, does not make her observations any less valid for social conflict. Burton (1990, pp. 2–3), more

generally, has defined resolution as 'the transformation of relationships in a particular case by the solution of the problems which led to
the conflictual behavior in the first place'. This definition of
resolution appears to be more general than the former, and its focus
is clearly on relationships between individuals. Perhaps the main
difference between the two definitions of resolution can be found in
the latter emphasis on transformation of relationships, whereas the
former takes no such line. In the former, the relationships may be
only one target of change; there may be other possible points of
attention in solving problems.

In the more narrow sense of resolution, processes are designed to
offer parties the opportunity to resolve should they wish to engage
in resolution. To some extent, processes are also designed to increase
the capacity of parties to resolve, either by emphasizing intellectual
techniques aimed at enhancing understanding, or by aiming to
improve the judgement of the parties. What no process can do,
however, is alter the world at large.

As an area of study, conflict resolution is a new phenomenon,
though it would be a mistake to say that nobody ever considered the
problem before Simmel and Coser. Most, if not all, political studies
involve the handling of conflict. The problem of social organization
and governance is one of how to handle, manage and ultimately to
resolve conflict. It is not, however, the task here to recapitulate the
centuries of work on the problem of social governance. Rather, the
objective is only to point to some key features that have salience for
the development of very specific types of resolution processes. It is
important to remember that the technologies of conflict resolution,
be they resolution through mediation or a problem-solving workshop, are all intellectually anchored. They come out of intellectual
traditions, some which are usually not associated with one another.
For example, the positivist tradition is reflected in many early
writings on the resolution of conflict, particularly those that were
found in the *Journal of Conflict Resolution*. It is sometimes wrongly
assumed that such traditions are not found in conflict resolution,
because of the alleged paradigm shift in the field. Even if the
paradigm shift has occurred, the intellectual traditions from which the
shift was made inform and influence the field. Of particular interest in
the study of conflict resolution is the intellectual tradition found in
democratic liberalism.

Democratic Liberalism and the Advent of Conflict Resolution

There can be little doubt that the philosophical underpinnings of democratic liberalism serve as the basis upon which much conflict resolution rests. This is interesting, because much of the analytical work done by those in conflict resolution does not explicitly come from this tradition. Whether democratic liberalism is in any way better than any other set of philosophical statements about the organization of life is debatable. Yet it appears that most processes of conflict resolution grow from and support the ideals of democratic liberalism. While this may be a contentious statement, I believe it is clearly supported by the facts.

Democratic liberalism grew from the eighteenth- and nineteenth-century writings of primarily British, French and American authors. With the rule of monarchs challenged, and vanquished first in Britain, then the fledgling USA and finally in France, there grew a movement to empower a new body to rule the maturing nation-state. Although there was among some a desire for democracy it was unclear what exactly that meant. The romantic version of a collection of citizens convening around an open courtyard to discuss and decide upon the matters of state gave way to those who distrusted their neighbours. Rather, the state was the embodiment of certain principles that were in need of protection. John Locke, the English philosopher, held that individuals must transfer their 'rights' of making and enforcing law to the state, which in exchange promised to uphold life and liberty. The requirement for the state to protect life and liberty exists because not all people are equally committed to protecting such. Therefore, the idea of an unfettered and totally free democratic state was never considered among the mainstream of political thought as a probability. Rather, democracy was required to offer certain protections against those who would transgress against others.

Thus, there appear to be certain 'rights' that must be protected by the state and there needs to be the surrender of a degree of individual autonomy to the state in order that these rights be protected. This same process is revealed in conflict resolution, where those at 'the table' come as representatives of others. They come in order that others may be represented and that certain 'rights' (values) may be protected. Although parties to a conflict resolution process must still return, and re-enter their social and organizational setting, they are to varying degrees still making some decisions for others. Even if specific agreements are not entered into, the range of possible areas of discussion certainly becomes limited simply through interaction. Parties, however, are not represented and protected for simple reasons of good neighbourliness. This is equally true of states; the protection of group members and citizens is involved.

The state did not protect life and liberty simply because these were good things (in part because 'good things' are particularly difficult to define). James Mill and Jeremy Bentham suggested that the state has another objective, as Held (1986, p. 15) explains:

> The key to their understanding of human beings, and of the system of governance most suited to them, lies in the thesis that humans act to satisfy desire and avoid pain. In brief their argument is as follows: the overriding motivation of human beings is to fulfil their desires, maximize their satisfactions or utilities, and minimize their suffering; society consists of individuals seeking as much utility as they can get from whatever it is they want; individuals' interests conflict with one another for 'a grand governing law of human nature', as Hobbes thought, is to subordinate 'the persons and properties of human beings to our pleasures'. Since those who govern will naturally act in the same way as the governed, government must, to avoid abuse, be directly accountable to an electorate called upon frequently to decide if their objectives have been met.

Thus, the state must not only control those under its sway, but be controlled by those whom it governs. It possesses the utilitarian objective of providing what Bentham called 'the greatest happiness of the greatest number'. The state does not exist to promulgate the interests of God, or of a particular class of people, or, on the surface, a particular ideology.

James Mill's son John Stuart Mill took things further, arguing that only through democracy, and the occasional and periodic mandate of the ruled, could good governance be achieved. The state could know whether it was maintaining the greatest good for the greatest number only if it asked the populace. Through voting, the state could maintain its legitimacy and could act in the name of the people, fostering their welfare and protecting their interests. Although it is unlikely that this is exactly what has happened over the past decades of liberal democracy, these were some of the ideas that were held in high esteem and which motivate the process of good governance today. The ethos of democratic liberalism informs not only governance, but all social relationships too.

What does this have to do with conflict resolution? While this is only the most cursory of outlines of democratic liberalism, most texts on conflict resolution would not even mention it. What modern conflict resolution has done is to replace many of the explanations of behaviour, such as the desire for life and liberty, with other motivations. For example, instead of arguing that people are motivated by the pursuit of life and liberty, Burton has argued that individuals are motivated out of needs satisfaction. He has replaced one set of motivations with a socio-biological explanation of human behaviour. Others have been less adventuresome in their scope, and have argued only that human motivations are based upon life and liberty, but that misperception stands in their way. Regardless of the motivations held, many of the objectives of conflict resolution remain the same as those in democratic liberalism. For example, most conflict resolution processes have within them some emphasis on the maintenance of legitimacy. John Stuart Mill's concept of polling to determine the popular support for government is echoed in asking those in conflict whether they concur with the resolution. In both settings the emphasis is upon the procedure, rather than on the substantive issues. Equally, conflict resolution is built around the idea of doing the greatest good for the greatest number. This is reflected in the concept of win–win outcomes, wherein an attempt is made to give all parties something of value.

The success of democratic liberal systems in resolving conflict is high, provided that there is a pre-existing consensus of values, or when the conflict centres on economics. Fukuyama (1992, pp. 117–18) comments that

> The success of American democracy at resolving conflicts between the various interest groups within its heterogeneous and dynamic population does not imply that democracy will similarly be able to resolve the conflicts that arise in other societies ... even American democracy has not been particularly successful in solving its most persistent ethnic problem, that of American blacks.

This suggests that the philosophical foundations upon which much of conflict resolution is built may not be up to supporting a strong conflict-resolving programme. The question which needs addressing is to what extent the failure of liberal democracy to resolve conflicts, with value dissensus, is a function of the philosophical foundations which inform it, and to what extent its failure is due to other factors.

A sign of some of the difficulties encountered by conflict resolution can be found in the recent attempts to export it to countries that do not share strong liberal values. In Eastern Europe, for example, liberalism has only recently, if at all, caught on. Some countries, like pre-World War II Czechoslovakia, had fledgling democratic institutions, but none with the same long evolution of liberal traditions as is found in the West. Going to the East, many conflict resolvers have found difficulty in having their programmes accepted. Ondrusek (1993) observes that complaints abound, such as people being overly reliant upon authority, misunderstanding the role of the mediator, or, according to Olszanska *et al.* (1993), expecting the mediator to be a high-status individual, as opposed to a skilled individual. Whether these difficulties are temporary, or of a more long-lasting nature, has yet to be seen. Most of the examples of the difficulties encountered in non-Western societies admittedly come from attempts at public conflict resolution, rather than private forums.

When we encounter other non-liberal traditions of conflict resolution, it is often striking just how alien they appear to those of a more liberal tradition. Take for example Wall and Blum's (1991) description of Chinese mediation. Unlike the Western notion of an independent, 'neutral' mediator, who sits between the parties, the Chinese process is characterized by an individual who seeks to suppress hostile feelings and one who takes sides in favour of the wronged party. Furthermore, mediation is not a voluntary social contract between disputants and a third party, as in the West, but rather it is compulsory for the good of the whole. Such a form of mediation would not sit well with the traditions of democratic liberalism.

As we move to examine some of the processes of conflict resolution in detail, it may well be worth keeping in mind their connection to the ideas of democratic liberalism. Some conflict-handling techniques are more closely tied to these ideals of democratic liberalism than others. Some processes of resolution are said to be value free, though they most likely reflect and uphold the values described here. Tillett (1990), for example, has outlined the many popular myths of mediation, many of which would have us believe that mediation is value free. What Tillett has done is ably to illustrate the value-laden nature of mediation. Many of the values defended in mediation are those of democratic liberalism, for example the emphasis on procedural fairness.

Not all theorists would agree that conflict resolution is value laden, be it mediation or problem-solving. Burton (1990, p. 204) writes, 'The third party is an observer in a scientific role. The third party makes no assessments, judgments or value interventions.'

Burton is among some theorists who view the resolution process as being largely process oriented and unconcerned with outcome. The tension between these two schools continues to be played out in the public forum of conflict resolution debates. What is interesting is that even those processes that are proclaimed to be value free contain within them the principles of democratic liberalism. Burton (ibid., p. 195), for example, argues 'that there must be full participation by the parties in any process dealing with the conflicts'. This emphasis upon all parties being represented in the resolution process is based partly upon the simple logic that if some parties are omitted from the process, then they may undercut it. This utilitarian approach – that is, providing the most to the greatest number – not only reflects the pragmatic interest of maintaining the process, but also nicely echoes democratic liberal ideas. Involvement of all parties also reflects John Stuart Mill's emphasis on polling the populace: involving all parties is comparable to Mill's emphasis upon voting; it ensures the legitimacy of the outcome.

Range of Processes

There is a range of processes used in attempts to handle social conflict. These include mediation, problem-solving workshops and facilitation, to name a few. There is some debate over whether a given process, mediation for example, is a conflict resolution process or a dispute resolution process. Recall that Burton distinguished between conflicts that concern values and needs, and disputes that are over interests. This dilemma has not been resolved here. Rather, it seems that there is adequate similarity in the roles and behaviours of third parties to warrant the inclusion of a variety of processes under the heading of conflict resolution. Two key behavioural similarities are the appearance of neutrality, and controlled communication. It will be useful to review these characteristics before moving on to an analysis of some of the more prominent processes.

Neutrality has long plagued conflict resolution processes, inasmuch as there are those who believe that a third party can be neutral, and those who believe otherwise. The question of whether a third party or a conflict resolution process is neutral carries considerable weight. If a process is in fact neutral then it ought to be able simply to receive information input from parties in conflict and generate a result, free from any ethical, belief or value judgements. The neutral process is analogous to a geologist conducting an experiment on a piece of rock. The geologist has no ethical or moral imperatives guiding the interaction with the rock, he or she simply studies it.

The expected neutrality of conflict resolution is premised upon the idea that a third party has no vested interest in the outcome of an intervention (be it a mediation or a problem-solving workshop). So, for example, in a community conflict two groups may be in conflict over expressions of racism; a third party may be called in. The third party would be from outside either community and not have any particular interest in the outcome. The two parties may exchange racial slurs, denounce one another, they may even threaten to engage in physical aggression against one another. Yet the neutral third party would only work towards some sort of resolution between the parties.

As might be expected, there are some difficulties with concept of neutrality. Perhaps the most obvious place to start is to recognize that a third party will certainly come to the table with a set of personal values and beliefs. No third party is neutral in every sense of the word, inasmuch as any third party carries his or her own set of values. So, for example, while the third party in the above example may not care about the racial slurs exchanged between the parties, he or she may care very deeply about racial slurs concerning his or her own group. Equally, a third party enters a conflict with some very clear ideas about the value of conflict and conflict resolution. A third party may be a committed pacifist, or may be less pacific. So, in a very real sense there is no person who is neutral. One's very actions and behaviours reflect one's own values and beliefs.

Marshall (1990, p. 120) believes that mediation, specifically, and I would add conflict resolution in general, 'determines certain forms of outcome. As "imposed" by mediators [or facilitators], the process is free of shows of physical aggression or abuse. It subtly predisposes toward cooperation and compromise'. Tillett (1990, p. 3) further argues that 'Mediation, and other forms of conflict resolution, are not value neutral.'

While it is impossible to say that any one person is in truth neutral, it must be noted that there is a real difference in behaviour between a third party and a combatant in conflict. Many who wish to debunk the thesis that conflict resolution is neutral go too far in their argument. There are some very real differences between parties in conflict and those who intervene, wishing to assist in resolution. For example, the third party will have a very different historical relationship with the parties. The third party will also have different institutional affiliations. Another noted difference between the third party and the combatants is that the third party, while not totally neutral, is quasi-neutral. Whereas those in conflict are absolutely not neutral, third parties wear a thin patina of neutrality. A third party may be neutral to the outcome and behaviours of the parties within a given range of acceptability. That range is defined by the third party's own values, by institutional values for the role of third party, as well as by her or his own ability to engage in rationalization. This rationalization would act to justify his or her own neutrality with respect to a given outcome or behaviour. Thus quasi-neutrality may be defined by a bastardized paraphrasing of Samuel Taylor Coleridge: one must engage in a willing suspension of belief and values. The third party does not become neutral; rather, he or she simply comes to pretend that they act as if they were neutral. Of course, such pretence will give way in times of stress, such as when core beliefs or values held by the third party are violated. In a hypothetical mediation of the Holocaust this pseudo-neutrality would have been sorely tested.

Just as conflict resolution processes employ a third party who engages in quasi-neutral behaviours, so too conflict resolution processes engage in controlled communication. Susskind and Cruikshank (1987) distinguish between unassisted and assisted negotiation: assisted negotiation employs the services of a third party in order to facilitate resolution. The authors suggest that a third party can overcome many of the difficulties experienced by parties to a conflict. Such difficulties may include complexity, high emotional, financial and/or psychological stakes, and finally power imbalances. Burton (1990) argues for the presence of a third party to control communication so that analysis may take place, and to help parties to a conflict move from bargaining behaviour to analytic behaviour. In any case, the third party takes control of the process of interactions between parties as the parties seek to resolve conflict. The scope of communication control is extreme, ranging from carrying messages between parties, such as in shuttle mediation, to forcing parties to restate and reconceptualize their messages, as found in problem-solving workshops.

For example, Folberg and Taylor (1984) write that mediation reduces hostility by encouraging direct communication. This encouragement can come only after the communication process between parties has been manipulated and controlled. The same feature also characterizes problem-solving workshops. Hill (1982) reviewed a variety of problem-solving workshops and concluded that the third party is essentially a facilitator who leads parties through the workshop process in order that they may come to a new definition of the conflict.

One of the key aims of controlled communication is attempting to assure that parties do not engage in misjudgement. As noted in Chapter 4, perception may be skewed depending upon how parties encounter a given event. If, for example, a negotiator is asked to select a selling price for a barrel of oil, the proposed range may influence that price selection. If a negotiator is offered a range of between $10 and $15, the difference may be split, resulting in a price of $12.50, whereas if a range of between $10 and $20 is offered, the difference may again be split, but this time resulting in a price of $15 per barrel. Controlled communication seeks to enhance judgement and guard against some of the predictable influences that result in misjudgement.

For a third party to engage in controlled communication and dictate the manner in which parties engage in discourse suggests that that third party has considerable power. This is true regardless of the type of conflict resolution process that is selected.

Of course, the control of communication puts into the hands of the third party a considerable degree of power. It also begs the question of third-party neutrality — after all, why would a neutral person wish to proscribe certain kinds of communication? The very fact that a third party can engage in the control of communication suggests that they possess a certain degree of power. Therefore, parties to the process must feel that they trust the third party. This raises some very interesting questions over values, ethics and beliefs. For example, a priest may have some difficulty in acting as a third party to a conflict if one of the parties to the conflict is an animist. Given the apparent ethical imperatives of the priest, the animist would probably be suspicious of the priest's motives. Of course, this can be answered in time, but it could take considerable effort on the part of the priest and the animist to come to an appropriate level of trust.

The Promise of Mediation

Bush and Folger (1994) have written an important book, *The Promise of Mediation*, that outlines differing views of what mediation is and what its value is. The authors argue that there are four primary objectives, or stories, found in mediation broadly. The first is the *satisfaction* story, wherein mediation serves to satisfy human needs.

This view of mediation is predicated upon mediation's 'flexibility, informality and consensuality' opening up 'the full dimensions of the problem facing the parties' (ibid., p. 16). Parties come to mediation because it is flexible, and thus convenient. Mediation is used because it is not adversarial, but rather seeks to satisfy the needs of the presenting parties.

A second story outlined by Bush and Folger is *social justice*. The social justice story emphasizes the role of mediation in the formation of community. Individuals, unattached to identified groups or interests, coalesce around interests discovered through the mediation process. Mediation, from the perspective of social justice, also helps create grassroots organizations that can solve local community problems. These problems were 'unsolvable' under former institutional arrangements. Community justice centres are examples of social justice mediation, where local community members serve as volunteer mediators solving local problems.

A third perspective or story in mediation is *transformation*. The value of mediation, from this viewpoint, is the ability to transform both individuals and society as a whole. The transformation story emphasizes real change of people and society, not simply the solution of problems. Transformation occurs because people truly alter their values and beliefs about themselves and others. They become empowered to solve their own problems. Bush and Folger (1994, p. 20) write:

> the private, nonjudgmental character of mediation can provide disputants a nonthreatening opportunity to explain and humanize themselves to one another. In this setting, and with mediators who are skilled at enhancing interpersonal communication, parties often discover that they can feel and express some degree of understanding and concern for one another despite their disagreement. ... Mediation has thus engendered, even between parties who start out as fierce adversaries, acknowledgment and concern for each other as fellow human beings.

Thus, the transformation story is one of optimism and hope.

Compare the optimism and hope with the *oppression* story. This story views mediation as a tool for control and domination. Even with the best of intentions, so goes this story, mediation can be used to obscure or deny procedural fairness. The cloak of confidentiality that often rings mediation keeps outsiders from looking in and evaluating what occurs against some social standard of fairness and equity. Thus mediation is a method for maintaining control by the powerful over the weak by obscuring and hiding conflicts.

Bush and Folger (1994) are advocates of the transformative value of mediation. They write:

> The strongest reason for believing that the Transformative Story should guide the mediation movement is the story's underlying premise: that the goal of transformation – that is, engendering moral growth toward both strength and compassion – should take precedence over the other goals mediation can be used to attain, even though those other goals are themselves important. (Ibid., pp. 28–9)

This is strong language. These authors' view of the transformative approach to mediation is a prescriptive one. It is not one of what currently goes on in mediation as such, but rather one of what should occur. Given this sort of advocacy, one must wonder about the troubled neutrality of the mediator. That aside, what Bush and Folger do in offering this prescriptive outline is underscore the depth of change required in order to obtain real social transformation. If racial hatred is not simply a personal aberration, but rather the result of a long-standing social process, then mediation must be transformative if it is to have an impact. The question Bush and Folger miss is whether mediation is a sufficiently analytical tool in the quest for social change.

From the above discussion it is at least clear that the conflict resolution process is not neutral or value free. Like the quasi-neutrality of the mediator, it may be that conflict resolution processes possess only a quasi-neutral appearance.

The Relative Presence of Value

The degree to which a process may be free from values imposed from outside is directly related to where the conflict takes place. As argued earlier, deep-rooted conflict may take place in any context, be it in an interpersonal relationship or between groups. The location of the deep-rooted conflict does, however, influence the manner in which it is dealt with. Waltz (1959) has argued that a major difference between the nation-state and the international system of states is that in the international arena there is no order, whereas within the state order exists. Within a nation-state, where governmental authority reigns, any given conflict resolution process must take into account the laws, values and morals which inform government. For example, a conflict resolution process which is intended to address racial conflict in the USA must take into account the laws of the local government, state government and federal government. Also necessary to account for are centrist values, pluralist representations and economic restrictions. These things not only must be taken into account in trying to understand a conflict, but directly influence the kind of process employed. It would be of little value in the USA to engage in a process that did not reflect the values of democratic liberalism. Processes that do not uphold such values, if such processes exist, would be rejected by many participants as being illegitimate, and might yield outcomes regarded as inappropriate for the political climate.

Domestic conflicts also bring greater pressure to bear on the resolution process than do international conflicts. Any given process that is immersed in a domestic environment must suffer the daily pressures of local media, interest groups and other key actors. Regardless of how secret a domestic process may be, local opinion will come to weigh heavily with those engaged in the process.

Although international conflicts are not free from these pressures and constraints, they are somewhat less affected. A key advantage found in international conflicts in escaping domestic pressures is found in the ability of the intervention team to leave the conflict environment. Thus the third party may escape some of the local pressures. Equally, since there is no value consensus in the international environment, third parties are less constrained by governmental values. Such international processes must still account for governmental values, just as the values of all participants must be kept in mind. Compared to domestic interventions, however, international interventions are somewhat freer from these constraints.

It will be useful to examine both domestic and international process to see how some of these pressures are found.

Communities in Conflict

There are many processes designed to assist with the resolution of community conflicts. These processes often focus on environmental and planning issues. There are a growing number of cases where governments are employing the services and techniques of those in conflict resolution. The processes employed in such attempts at resolving community conflict include negotiation, mediation and facilitation. Yet rather than focus on technique, the objective here is to suggest that these processes reflect the general argument above that conflict resolution processes are not value free and are largely connected to the values of democratic liberalism. As argued above, because these approaches take place within the borders of a nation-state, they are constrained by the degree to which they may stray from the dictates of a given national leadership.

Susskind and Cruikshank (1987) argue that positive community conflict resolution outcomes are characterized by fairness, efficiency, wisdom and stability. The authors argue that key in defining fairness are the perceptions of the participants to the process. Thus an outcome is considered fair if the parties judge it so, regardless of community interests at large. Presumably, then, parties who may be happy to live in unstable, criminal or destructive relationships are acceptable. Another key is efficiency, which can be described as any cuts in expenditure of time over what would have been expended in a different setting. Wisdom is rather ambiguous and seems to operate to prevent bad outcomes. It refers to that which the parties should be reasonably expected to know, given their experience and knowledge base. Finally, the authors identify stability as being the final component of a good outcome. Stability refers to the long-term endurance of an outcome. Even a fair, efficient and wise outcome is doomed to failure if it is such that it will not endure the test of time.

The four characteristics outlined here, however, are also those which are conservative. While there may be nothing wrong with a conservative outcome, it suggests that such domestic processes are limited in the degree to which they may change conditions influencing a given conflict. For example, if the dismantling of a nuclear power plant is perceived as the best way of reducing a local conflict, it still may not happen if it is perceived by the political leadership to be contrary to their interests. It is government that has the ability and capacity, more so than other groups, to destabilize an agreement, or create inefficiencies in the face of unacceptable agreements. Thus most attempts at resolving community conflicts are within the established and political elite framework. Of course, those who advocate these processes are well aware of their position *vis-à-vis* government. As Crowfoot and Wondolleck (1990, p. 13) note, 'Environmental [and other community processes] negotiation and mediation are merely a recent extension and refinement of the long-established practice of informal negotiation among differing interest groups and individuals.' As adjuncts to existing forms of governance, these approaches take an analytical approach only within the existing confines of the political system. This acts to further curtail the range of possible outcomes.

Problem-solving Workshops

The problem-solving workshop grows out of several intellectual traditions and has found its place in the world of conflict resolution. Unlike mediation, however, the problem-solving workshop has not experienced the same fantastic growth in popularity. Perhaps this is because such workshops require greater institutional support and cannot be done by a lone third party, as mediation can.

Two different approaches to the problem-solving workshop are considered here. Burton has been a leader of the use of these processes in the international arena. He brings to the workshop a set of unique and inventive ideas about the origins of conflict and the methods for resolution. Also examined is work undertaken by Vamik Volkan and the Center for the Study of the Mind and Human Interaction. Volkan's approach, while equally inventive, is more deeply steeped in the traditions of psychoanalytic theory. Examining both approaches will offer some interesting insights into the methods of resolution. Characteristic of both workshop approaches is a commitment to a problem-solving logic. Banks and Mitchell (1996, p. 5) write:

> Any problem-solving initiative starts, continues and concludes with some third party devoting its attention to the interests of *all* [emphasis original] the parties in a given dispute, as determined by those parties themselves. It involves the principle of putting adversaries in a situation where they can explore the possibilities for new options leading to a 'win–win', or variable sum solution to what can be recognized as a mutual problem. A major task for the third party is not to use leverage nor to search for a bargained compromise, but the provision of a safe venue in which productive discussions might take place, maximizing the chances of a genuine exchange of ideas, of free-ranging analysis and of the non-committing exploration of options.

There is variation between workshops, but they share many of the similarities described here.

The problem-solving workshop evolved in the 1960s. Such workshops often grew out of similar processes found in psychology, for example, the T-group. Burton, Doob and Kelman have been the pioneers of the problem-solving workshop, as conducted on international conflict. Intellectually, the workshops find a direct link with the work of Kurt Lewin and action research. Academics and others have taken Lewin's original idea of linking diagnosis to training to social change, and have modified it to fit somewhat different circumstances. Problem-solving workshops, according to Hill (1982), have two objectives. The first is 'to provide conflict researchers with an opportunity to investigate the dynamics of an ongoing international conflict' and the second is to 'provide a setting in which the parties to the conflict could meet and learn techniques that would enable them to resolve eventually the conflict peacefully' (p. 111). The manner in which these processes have been implemented has varied from case to case. They share, however, some substantial areas of commonality, such as those outlined by Burton and Dukes (1990), including the breaking of conflicts down into parties and issues; face-to-face interaction between the parties and a third party; use of facilitators; and intense analytical discussions. Of particular interest is the common feature among the different varieties of workshop in being analytical, rather than merely facilitative (as in mediation).

Burton has written extensively on the use of the problem-solving workshop and how it may be employed to resolve conflicts. The workshop, as envisioned by Burton, consists of a panel of experts in conflict resolution, and parties to the conflict representing the various sides and factions. The parties are not themselves officials of the government, *per se*, but rather significant persons from that party – that is, they are knowledgeable about the conflict and about the group from which they come. The workshops are held in secret, in order that no outside pressures may be brought to bear on the parties as they proceed through the process. The objective of the process is analytical and not negotiative.

Intellectually, Burton's workshop is quite different from other processes, such as mediation or arbitration. Several characteristics, argues Burton, separate the problem-solving workshop from other, more conventional conflict-handling techniques. First, the problem-solving workshop is not driven by the aim of obtaining a terminal solution, but rather its object is to bring about a new set of relationships between the parties. Recall Burton's definition of resolution as the transformation of relationships between parties. In changing the relationships between parties one is not necessarily creating conditions where no conflict will exist, but ones where the new relationships put to rest the old conflict. The new relationships may, over time, come to find new conflict, but hopefully this will be less destructive than the prior sort.

Second, Burton (1990, p. 202) argues that 'problem-solving frequently requires a new synthesis of knowledge, new techniques and a change in conceptualization of a problem'. Explanations of behaviour must be challenged in order that creative solutions may be obtained. Creative solutions are not an end in themselves, but rather highlight the likelihood that old ways of solving problems were inadequate. Burton often sites deviance as an example of where new conceptualization of problems is needed. For Burton, deviance is often a sign of an individual attempting to meet unmet needs. Deviance cannot be solved by coercion, but rather is solved by attempting to examine why persons behave as they do, and attempting to come up with a new set of relationships which will meet the needs of the individual.

Third, Burton holds that problem-solving must focus on the entirety of human relationships in order fully to address and comprehend the problem faced. In this, Burton is arguing that one cannot excise a problem from its social setting; a problem can be understood only in context and in relation to everything else. For example, the resolving of an environmental dispute must take into account not only those directly affected by the problem, but also those affected by any would-be resolution. Workers at the chemical manufacturing plant many kilometres away from the spot of the environmental problem are as much part of the process as the citizens directly affected. Equally, government policy, technological change and a host of other forces and actors, in Burton's schema, would need to be considered.

Fourth, Burton (1990, p. 203) argued that 'to be effective problem-solving goes back to sources and origins' of the conflict. It is not enough in an environmental conflict to bargain over how much dangerous chemical is released into the atmosphere, but it is necessary to understand why the chemical is needed, how that need came about, why that particular chemical was selected, and why it is released into the atmosphere. To bargain only over how much dangerous chemical may be released is to beg the question. The chemical will still be released, and there is always the possibility that its release will increase over time as new economic and social pressures come to bear. Bargaining often only puts off the inevitable, whereas problem-solving aims to bring about a true solution.

Burton's problem-solving workshops have been employed in a variety of settings throughout the world. Reportage of the outcome of these workshops is difficult to unearth, however. More widely reported, however, has been the work of Volkan and its outcomes.

Volkan, a psychiatrist by training, has developed a problem-solving workshop that is designed

> not to resolve the conflict, but to create an environment in which the psychological barriers that so often impede official diplomacy can rise to the surface, be discussed openly, and then be taken into account in the negotiations of 'real world' political issues. (Volkan and Harris, 1992, p. 24)

He has written a number of pieces that provide the reader with an insight into the actual workings of specific conflict interventions.

The approach used by Volkan consists of an interdisciplinary team, though one where everybody has a basic understanding of psychoanalysis and psychodynamics. As is true of Burton's process, Volkan and Harris (1992) emphasize that such meetings should be unofficial in nature, and not designed to yield a given outcome. Rather, it is argued that what may be most important is an airing of historical grievance, so that parties may be heard, and the chance to get ideas 'in the air'. In this way ideas are floated, yet without attribution or ownership.

There are four key ideas employed by Volkan and Harris (1992):

1. the awareness that events have more than one meaning, and that sometimes a hidden meaning is more important than a surface one;
2. that all interactions, whether they take the form of overt or concealed actions, verbal or non-verbal statements, formal or informal gatherings, are meaningful and analysable;
3. that the initiation of a process in which problems become the 'shared problems' of opposing parties is more essential than the formulation of 'logical' or 'quick' answers; and
4. that the creation of an atmosphere in which the expression of emotions is acceptable can lead to the recognition of underlying resistances to change.

It is important to note that Volkan has diverged dramatically from what many might believe to be the international negotiation ideal, where parties sit around a table acting the part of the cool diplomat. He has emphasized the emotional, or affective, aspect of any given conflict.

Volkan's work differs in some ways from that of others, but it also shares similarities. For example, Volkan and Burton share some important commonalities. Aside from using the workshop format, they both emphasize the analysis of statements and behaviour, seeking some more deeply held meaning than what appears on the surface. This emphasis on analysis and understanding the dynamics of conflict is tempered by Volkan (1979), who argues, 'it must be remembered that understanding a problem may help one solve it, but understanding per se provides no solution' (p. 30). Equally, both workshop formats depend upon parties coming to recognize that they share problems, the resolution to which must come interdependently. Once again, it should be noted that sharing a problem may help in resolution, but it is not a solution in itself. Where Volkan and Burton diverge is primarily around the kind of analysis undertaken. Volkan's process borrows concepts from psychoanalysis and psychology, whereas Burton's concepts are in part borrowed and in part developed by him. Burton attempts to develop a coherent set of theoretical statements about human conflict behaviour, whereas Volkan depends more on traditional psycho-analytic theory.

There are many other types of problem-solving processes. Some, like those of Burton and Volkan, focus on questions of deep sources of motivation, whereas others are more concerned with the question of judgement and processes of decision making. All processes, however, regardless of whether their focus is motivation or judgement, must be concerned with the issue of power.

Problem, Power and Process

A key advantage of the problem-solving workshop approach is that it cuts beneath the surface of the conflict to deal with its more profound sources. Mediation, for example, often addresses only the surface issues, as presented by the parties, instead of identifying the deeper motivations underlying the issues. Where some processes would omit important factors in consideration of the conflict, the problem-solving format includes them. Yet as was noted earlier, the mere fact of cutting deeply into a conflict does not make it necessarily any easier to resolve. Depth of understanding should not be equated with ease of resolution.

Anstey provides a long list of criticisms concerning the problem-solving workshop, writing:

> The problem-solving approach has in turn been criticised as ignoring or dealing superficially with the issue of power realities in relationships, the

problem of scarce resources which prohibit integrative solutions even where parties are aware of each others' needs and interests, and the fact that meeting needs of identity, recognition, and development may have very real and negative implications for the security and identity of other groups, not to mention their economic welfare. In addition a particular group's identity may reside in the use of adversarial tactics – it needs conflict more than it needs settlement. Struggle groups practised in adversarial skills may feel far stronger fighting than they do in a negotiation situation. Where coercive strategies have won higher wages, new rights, and political influence, struggle groups may be reluctant to relinquish these for the uncertainties of joint problem-solving – especially if they perceive the other party to be better equipped, in terms of education, skills, and control over existing resources, for the alternative approach. Leaders who arise in struggle situations may be good generals, but may lack the vision or capacity to participate effectively in nation-building initiatives. Thus alternative approaches to negotiation may be far more difficult to implement than a superficial reading of the literature would imply. (Anstey, 1993, pp. 77–8)

This clearly brings out the difficulties found when the issue of power comes into play. Groups in conflict are engaged in the exercise of power. Although they may not, ultimately, be seeking to engage in conflict for the sake of power, they nonetheless are quite practised in the art of using and responding to power. Some groups are unable to alter their social situation without using the tools of power, in order to multiply and augment their resources. Workers strike and withhold their labour in an effort to gain power; racial minorities engage in protests and marches; others engage in planting bombs. These struggle groups gain access to the negotiation or problem-solving process because they have exercised power. If the process of resolution takes away a group's means of empowerment, then that struggle group will leave the process. This, then, begs the question as to whether the process is at all effective.

What a process, such as Volkan's, may unearth is that a group exists because of the conflict, and because of one group's opposition to its enemy. Removing the enemy, effectively curing a group, may also lead to its undoing. If this threat to group identity is perceived, then that group may leave the process. For example, the Ku Klux Klan, who enmify African Americans, would hardly wish to be cured of its enmification if the leaders also perceived that it would mean an end to the group. In fact, this is the most difficult area for conflict resolution, namely how to navigate through the difficult course of power relationships.

Susskind and Cruikshank may write about the characteristics of a good agreement as being fairness, efficiency, wisdom and stability, but it is quite another thing to see those through to the end. As noted above, governments or other powerful actors can easily interfere with the process of obtaining fair, efficient, wise or stable agreements. Equally, the powerful can interfere with problem-solving workshops that seek to discover either unmet human needs or deeply seated psychological processes. Thus as conflict resolution processes are discussed, parties must be in a situation where any party that can effectively stymie the process must be in agreement that the process should proceed.

The outcome of processes which are boycotted (a form of power) by a given party are profoundly skewed, and often unworkable. In Cambodia, the Khmer Rouge were partly omitted from and partly boycotted the peace process led by the UN. As a result, while many had proclaimed the resolution process in Cambodia to have been a success, the Khmer Rouge continued to arm, train military cadres and plan for battle. Thus the Khmer Rouge were effectively wielding considerable power as they attempted to undermine the peace process. Anstey's comment above about struggle groups is pertinent here: the Khmer Rouge gained power from the barrel of the gun, and without the gun they stood to lose their power base.

In Ireland the dynamic of power and the peace process is played out in a variety of ways. It is likely that the IRA gain far more attention for their position than they would if it were not for their use of violence. Thus the laying down of arms is problematic for them. To stop armed struggle and surrender their weapons leaves them with few means of gaining attention for their cause. Whether the peace process in Northern Ireland works is, of course, not just a matter of what the IRA does, but also one of what the British government elects to do. So, in the early 1990s the British government engaged in secret, and later not so secret, talks with the IRA. Yet the government was in control, being able publicly to set conditions and the agenda of talks. This is because it holds the instruments of power found in all modern states: a police force, an army, an intelligence service and virtual control of the media. It would appear that no matter how many bombs the IRA explode, they will never be able to match the power of the nation-state.

This does not all mean, however, that states or others in power are impervious to influence. The British have engaged in a peace process precisely because the exercise of power alone does not ensure growth and harmony. 'The Troubles' of Northern Ireland create enormous hardship for British taxpayers, stifle economic growth and create ongoing havoc for the UK generally. Political leaders, the elite and others cannot long ignore other stresses and strains on society, nor can they perpetuate a reliance on power as a cure-all for such situations. The USA discovered that military power was insufficient to win the Vietnam War, and the leaders of the former USSR discovered that totalitarian states that wield the club of power against their own people are also destined to fail.

Thus it appears that there is a dynamic tension between power and other forces. Effective conflict resolution can be derailed by the exercise of power, yet power by itself is rarely enough to resolve conflict. It is a mistake, in discussing conflict resolution processes, to ignore power. Yet it is equally a mistake to believe that just because the state has a monopoly of power, the leadership will never engage in a resolution process.

Conclusion: Processes in Question

It appears clear that no matter what process is employed, conflict is guided and influenced by a variety of factors. Such factors, like power, are sufficiently pervasive that they can barely be curtailed or controlled. Yet some of the influences of power, for example, can be mitigated by skilled and thoughtful intervention. The desire to find the right formula or right process is largely a chimera, however. Processes can help overcome some of the negative influences of misjudgement, but they are less useful when trying to overcome the difficulties presented by power.

Different processes have, of course, different objectives. Some are more useful in some circumstances than others. Volkan's stressing of the psychological may be of particular use in an environment where violence has already passed, and the emphasis is upon 'national healing'. Burton's approach to resolution, unlike Volkan's, is designed more for long-term planning than for long-term healing.

It should be clear, however, that processes can have only a limited impact upon the resolution of conflict. Events in the environment at large play a larger role than anything that happens within the mediation session or problem-solving workshop. Parties who expect reasonable results from their involvement with a conflict resolution process would be well advised to consider to what extent they can control events in general. Any party has only limited control over their capacity to resolve, and this is equally true of the opportunity to resolve. Perhaps what is most notable when parties engage in a resolution process is the simple fact that they seek resolution. This in itself represents for many parties a considerable shift in focus. Regardless of the type of process in question, it will be important for the prospective parties to carefully consider the type of process and whether it will work in a given context.

References

Anstey, Mark (1993) *Practical Peacemaking*. Kenwyn, South Africa: Juta and Co.

Banks, Michael and Christopher Mitchell (1996) *Handbook of Conflict Resolution*. London: Pinter.

Burton, John (1990) *Conflict: Resolution and Prevention*. New York: St Martin's Press.

Burton, John and Frank Dukes (1990) *Conflict: Practices in Management, Settlement and Resolution*. New York: St Martin's Press.

Bush, Robert A. Baruch and Joseph P. Folger (1994) *The Promise of Mediation*. San Francisco: Jossey-Bass.

Crowfoot, James E. and Julia M. Wondolleck (1990) *Environmental Disputes*. Washington, DC: Island Press.

Folberg, Jay and Alison Taylor (1984) *Mediation*. San Francisco: Jossey-Bass.

Fukuyama, Francis (1992) *The End of History and the Last Man*. New York: The Free Press.

Heitler, Susan (1990) *From Conflict to Resolution*. London: W.W. Norton and Co.

Held, David (1986) 'Introduction: Central Perspectives on the Modern State', in David Held *et al.* (eds) *States and Societies*. London: Open University.

Hill, Barbara (1982) 'An Analysis of Conflict Resolution Techniques', *Journal of Conflict Resolution* 26(1), 109–38.

Marshall, Tony (1990) 'The Power of Mediation', *Mediation Quarterly* 8(2), 115–24.

Olszanska, Justyna, Robert Olszanski and Jacek Wozniak (1993) 'Do Peaceful Conflict Management Methods Pose Problems in Posttotalitarian Poland?', *Mediation Quarterly* 10(3), 291–302.

Ondrusek, Dusan (1993) 'The Mediator's Role in National Conflicts in Post-Communist Central Europe', *Mediation Quarterly* 10(3), 246–7.

Susskind, Lawrence and Jeffrey Cruikshank (1987) *Breaking the Impasse*. New York: Basic Books.

Tillett, Greg (1990) 'Myths of Mediation', Centre for Conflict Resolution, Discussion Paper Series. Sydney: Macquarie University.

Volkan, Vamik (1979) *Cyprus: War and Adaptation*. Charlottesville: University Press of Virginia.

Volkan, Vamik and Max Harris (1992) 'Negotiating a Peaceful Separation: A Psychopolitical Analysis of Current Relationships between Russia and the Baltic Republics', *Mind and Human Interaction* 4(1), 20–39.

Wall, James A. and Michael Blum (1991) 'Community Mediation in the People's Republic of China', *Journal of Conflict Resolution* 35(1), 3–20.

Waltz, Kenneth (1959) *Man, the State, and War*. New York: Columbia University Press.

9
WHERE TO FROM HERE?

In the preceding chapters considerable emphasis has been placed upon factors that impinge upon conflict. Some are embedded within individual psychology, whereas others are entrenched in social systems. Still other factors lie somewhere in between. Yet all these factors play a common role in influencing the course of conflict, and affect the ease with which conflict is resolved. In light of what has been addressed thus far, consider again how the necessary and sufficient conditions of conflict resolution may be impacted.

Capacity

The capacity to resolve a conflict refers to ability. The ability to resolve is influenced by many factors. For example, many organizations have concluded that training individuals in conflict resolution skills can offset the high levels of organizational conflict. Employees receive training in effective communication skills, problem-solving skills and mediation, for example. Upon critical analysis, however, one may come to question the impact of such training. In a workplace environment affected by racism there is some real concern over just how useful effective communication skills will be. What will be communicated effectively? Will it be messages of amity and peace, or enmity and hate? Training individuals in communication carries with it the assumption that people will communicate in ways that enhance relationships. Yet we know that communication is as much about communicating cooperation as it is about communicating competition. Language is power laden and therefore can be used to disempower or empower, depending upon the disposition of the person using it.

Structural factors also influence the capacity to resolve conflict. Social inequities and imbalances of power impact upon those who would resolve conflict. The requisite education necessary to talk about and resolve some environmental conflicts may well be beyond the existing capacity of some. Many conflicts between indigenous people and ruling cultures reflect this particular structural problem. These structural factors are often mired in the histories of groups and people, and overcoming history is a long and arduous process.

Creating capacity may be something as simple as training a group of workers in effective conflict resolution skills. It may also be something far grander, entailing the education of the entire society. Such large-scale efforts may be not only large, but also long in time. Creating sufficient capacity may require educating several generations in order to create sufficient capacity.

Unfortunately, most conflict resolution efforts seem to focus almost exclusively upon changing the capacity of individuals, rather than focusing on a whole range of factors. By omitting other aspects of conflict, conflict resolution efforts focusing exclusively on capacity create false expectations of success, while leaving parties under-resourced to deal with the conflict at hand.

Opportunity

Opportunity refers to possessing the chance to resolve. Do people have enough time to resolve conflict? Are they able to interact? Creating opportunity for resolution is the motivation behind many peacekeeping operations. Separating warring parties provides time for each to consider their options and begin the process of dialogue. A variety of factors prevent the development of opportunity. At the most basic level is time. Is there enough time to resolve a given conflict? In the midst of a shouting argument time may not be present, but methods can be pursued to create time.

Structural factors also exist that prevent the opportunity to resolve. For example, a low-caste Indian is unlikely even to receive the opportunity to talk to Brahmins. Thus resolving India's long-running domestic problems becomes virtually impossible. Of course, symbolic inhibitions to the creation of opportunity also abound. History creates real problems in resolution. Parties may come to believe that the other side will not offer the opportunity to resolve. 'Why even bother talking to them, we already know they won't budge' is an oft-heard comment from parties in conflict. History and belief serve to create symbolic blocks to the creation of opportunity.

It is healthy that on the international front there is some interest in working out problems associated with peacekeeping. In seeking to work out these problems, members of the international community have come to recognize the importance of opportunity in resolution. Domestically, the situation is less promising. There seems little interest in creating the opportunity to resolve domestic conflicts, such as US race relations. One of the difficulties of creating such opportunities is that often one party or another has a vested interest in maintaining the social structure the way it is. Creating an opportunity to resolve may put at jeopardy profitable social structures.

Volition (Will)

Creating the will to resolve is perhaps one of the most difficult problems in the whole study of conflict resolution. Zartman and Berman (1982, p. 66) write, 'Without the will to reach agreement there will be none.' One often hears the refrain, 'Yes, but what if they don't want to resolve?' Parties can be skilled in the language and analytical tools of resolution, opportunities for dialogue may abound, yet at the end if parties do not wish to engage in resolution, then there is little that can be done.

Burton (1988) has tried to focus on this problem of volition by suggesting that parties be encouraged to cost the conflict. Such costing may lead parties to assess their current behaviour and undertake actions leading to a de-escalation of the conflict. Of course, trying to get parties to cost their behaviour is easier said than done. Parties may also err in their costing, and use a costing exercise as an excuse to rationalize their existing position.

One of the great challenges in seeking to create the will to resolve is the existence of history. The ideological formation of history serves to explain and justify current behaviour. A divorced couple each explain the continuation of enmity not on the basis of current behaviour, but rather upon the history of their relationship. No will to resolve can emerge from that relationship while parties are locked into seeing the world with historical eyes.

Coercion, threats and power all are methods that have been used in the past to force parties in resolving conflict. They each have their limits and have proven over time to be very inefficient. Each can bring parties together falsely and in bad faith. Talks may happen, agreements may be struck, but while the head is in the negotiations, the heart is on the battlefield. Creating the will to resolve means more than simply bringing parties together to talk; it means bringing parties together so that they may enter into a real conflict resolution dialogue. Not surprisingly, creating such a will is very difficult indeed.

Conclusion

Throughout the preceding chapters a critical emphasis has been placed upon the processes that impact upon the resolution of conflict. Metaphorically, it is as if people are permeated by a spider's web, or connected by countless invisible webs that link one another's past and present, and which influence the course of their behaviour. Accounting for these webs is the task of any who wish to resolve conflict, for without an understanding of how they pull and tug at those in conflict, resolution is condemned to failure. Simplistic models of human behaviour, of social organization or of conflict will doom any process of resolution.

At the outset it was argued that there were three necessary and sufficient conditions to resolution: volition (will), opportunity and capacity. In this book the ways in which these elements are constrained by events and forces well outside the control of the individual have been examined. No matter what skills or processes are brought to bear upon a conflict, there is still the remainder of the world to impact upon the process:

In the 1950s, Timothy Leary (prior to his rise to popular fame and infamy) conducted research on psychotherapy to see whether talk therapy worked. Running an experimental and a control group, he discovered that in the control group one-third of the patients got well, one-third stayed the same and one-third were worse off. The experimental group was exactly the same: one-third recovered, one-third stayed the same and the other third became worse. What this suggested was that either what psychologists did did not work, or there were many other variables which influenced an individual and which were beyond the control and influence of the psychologist. Throughout this book it has been argued that conflict resolution is constrained by the same social forces that constrain the psychologist. This is not to say that the psychologist should have surrendered then and there, but rather, the need to identify areas where a difference could be made seemed the most appropriate step.

The study of conflict resolution is in much the same condition. Third parties must ask where a difference can be made, while recognizing the historical and psychological powers with which conflicts are invested. Overcoming generations of enmity is a tall order, even for the most skilled third party. Perhaps it will be found that resolution results in one-third of the conflicts worsening, one-third staying the same and one-third being resolved.

One of the key impediments to effective resolution is articulating a rationale for resolution. Simmel argued that resolution acts to unify disunity. Thus there is a constructive, positive aspect to conflict. Yet this is only from one perspective and is value laden. When is a conflict constructive, when is it destructive? There is no value-free, 'scientific' equation that can be operated to discover this. One expected many conservative, nationalist Afrikaners to believe that a fight to the death, in order to save the Boer nation, would be a good conflict. Others strongly disagreed, and saw a powerful role for conflict resolution. What this suggests is that both scholars and practitioners need to develop a clearly articulated value basis upon which to build their work, or they must discover the scientifically value-neutral equation which can differentiate between constructive conflicts and destructive ones. The former is possible (and already exists to some extent), but may not be useful for the long-term development of a culturally sensitive discipline. The latter is unlikely. Most theorists in conflict resolution, either implicitly or explicitly, identify destructive conflict as the target of resolution processes. Yet few theorists provide an explicit method by which one can determine what are constructive and what are destructive conflicts.

It must be remembered that conflict is not a discrete event in life, but rather informs and influences everything people do. The language spoken, the friends kept, alliances and enemies – all are part of the process of conflict. Separating the good aspects from the bad is like separating grains of sand: the grains keep shifting, are very hard to distinguish, and it takes an awfully long time. If one reflects on just how deeply ingrained conflict is in life one may be surprised. Some might be struck by just how many 'French' jokes can be heard in England. These jokes are born of enmity and conflict, and although there is no (or little) conflict between the French and English today, the history of past conflict lives on. Southern Americans who speak with the characteristic drawl are still castigated and looked down upon by many as being slow and stupid. This stereotype persists despite such brilliant Southern writers as William Faulkner, Truman Capote, Tennessee Williams and William Penn Warren, to name a few. Yet the American Civil War still carries its weight today in the stereotype of Southerners.

These two examples are small illustrations of the ways in which conflict intrudes into our daily lives.

What this suggests is that conflict resolution is a difficult process. Burton is correct in asserting the ascendancy of theory over practice. All the practice in the world does not create a power-free, level playing-field. Only by understanding the dynamics of conflict and resolution can a third party, or the parties themselves, have a hope of resolving conflict. Yet theory alone cannot carry the day either. Theory cannot overcome all obstacles, though it can help us understand them. While Burton is correct to put theory where he does, it would be wrong to think for a moment that all conflicts can, one day, be totally resolved. The very best we can hope is that the number of conflicts can be reduced, and that their duration will be far shorter than is the case today.

The mood need not be all doom and gloom for the future of conflict resolution. The field has progressed markedly in the past twenty years. Conflict resolution can work, and it can be effective. What is required, however, is a recognition that many conflicts have existed for decades, if not centuries. Given the length of time of these conflicts, and the costs incurred, it would be overly idealistic to believe that there exists some process whereby conflicts can be resolved in a relatively short span of time. What needs recognition is that the process of resolution relies upon the intellectual and communicative skill of all parties (third party and otherwise), the willingness of those in conflict to resolve, and the general cooperation of events which may influence the course of resolution. It is not enough to have two out of three of these requirements for resolution to take place; all three must be present.

Sisyphus was condemned to roll a stone up a hill, only to have the gods conspire against him and have the stone roll back down. No matter what Sisyphus did, he could not lodge the stone permanently atop the hill, for it always rolled back down. Conflict resolution can become similarly Sisyphean if caution is not used. The gods, those unseen powers, force the stone off the peak and back down into the valley. For conflict resolution, those gods are the influences of history, the psychology of individuals, the actions of unrelated parties. Care must be taken to recognize those forces so that processes may be designed, and expectations harboured, which are appropriate to the situation. All of this can be done. What is needed, though, is a clear-headed recognition of those forces.

References

Burton, John (1988) *Conflict Resolution as a Political System*. Working Paper 1. Fairfax, Virginia: Center for Conflict Analysis and Resolution, George Mason University.

Zartman, William I. and Maureen R. Berman (1982) *The Practical Negotiator*. New Haven, CT: Yale University Press.

INDEX

action research   67, 69, 74
adjudication   22–3
Afrikaners   112–14, 117, 121, 134, 175
aggression   43–9, 51–7, 75
alienation   133–5
Allport, Gordon   65
alternative dispute resolution
   (ADR)   15–17, 37
altruism   45
anchoring   92, 93
Anstey, Mark   165–6
anti-language   98
arbitration   19, 20, 22, 23, 162
Ardrey, Robert   45–6
Argyris, Chris   61
Australian Family Court   15–16
availability   92, 93–4
Avruch, Kevin   80–1
Axelrod, Robert   71

Bandura, Albert   54–5
Bay of Pigs, Cuba   116–17
behavioural decision theory   92, 94
Bentham, Jeremy   150
Bercovitch, Jacob   33, 34
Beyond Machiavelli   24
Black, Peter   80–1
Blake, Robert   11, 108
Boulding, Kenneth   14
bounded rationality   107
Burke, Edmund   42
Burke, Kenneth   64, 90
Burton, John   8–9, 12–13, 20, 38, 39, 41,
   56–7, 60, 74, 75, 77–81, 105, 108,
   117–19, 135, 142, 144, 145, 151,
   152–3, 155, 161, 162–3, 164, 165,
   168, 173, 176
Bush, Robert   156–8

capacity   4–5, 6, 88, 148, 160, 168, 171–
   2, 174
Carnevale, Peter   20, 80
Center for the Study of Mind and Human
   Interaction   161
Centre for the Analysis of conflict
   (CAC)   13

Chomsky, Noam   91
Churchill, Winston   96
Coleridge, Samuel Taylor   155
communication   84, 86–106,
   108–10, 117
   controlled   155–6
   defined   89
   in groups   94–9
Community Justice Centres   16
conciliation   21, 27
conflict
   analysis   120–3
   approach–avoidance   66
   in communities   159–61
   deep-rooted   37–41, 74, 136, 142,
      143, 158
   defined   30–6
   intractable   38–9, 74, 136
   management   38
   in organizations   10–12, 120, 171
   settlement   38
   and time   36–7
   transformation   72–4
Conflict   62
conflict resolution
   defined   147–8
   history of   8–17
Conflicts   24
contingency theories   41, 134
Control: The Basis of Social Order   78
Coser, Lewis   33, 63–5, 69, 70, 72, 83,
   126, 128–9, 133, 142, 148
Crichton, Michael   19
Cuban missile crisis   115–17

De Bono, Edward   24, 25
de Waal, Frans   46–8
decision-making   92–4, 115–17, 165
deep-rooted conflict, *see under* conflict
dehumanization   136–8
democratic liberalism   148–53, 159, 160
Deutsch, Morton   31, 67–9, 70, 81–4,
   105, 133
Disclosure   19
Dollard, John   51–2
Doob, Leonard   13, 51, 161

Eight Essential Steps to Conflict Resolution 26
Eliade, Mircea 103
enemies 46, 126–45, 166
  biological origin of 130–3
  enemy system 139–42
  nature of 128–30
  social origins of 133–5
enmity
  historical, defined 141
  intragroup 143–4
espoused theories 61
ethnocentrism 142–3
Evolution of Cooperation 71
exchange theories 99

Federal Meditation and Conciliation Service (USA) 21
field theory 65–7
Fights, Games and Debates 38
final offer arbitration 22
Fisher, Roger 24, 25, 26
Folger, Joseph 156–8
Follett, Mary Parker 10, 11
Freud, Sigmund 42–3, 44
frustration 51–2
frustration–aggression hypothesis 52
Frustration and Aggression 51
functional theories of conflict 32, 33
Functions of Social Conflict 33, 63

Galbraith, John Kenneth 1
Galton's error 55–6
Galtung, Johann 32, 34
game theory 69–72, 74, 82, 84, 126
Getting to Yes 8
groups
  defined 94
  functional 111–12
  human 111–12
  leaders in 95–6
  maintenance function 95
  task function 95

heuristics 92–4
Hill, Barbara 13–14
history 107–24
  defined 109
Hobbes, Thomas 36, 42, 48, 49, 150
Holocaust, the 128

identity 96–8, 103, 115, 118, 135–6, 142, 144, 166
ideology 104, 109, 143, 144
  defined 104
inherency theories 41, 42–8, 55, 56, 134

interactionist theories of conflict 33, 34, 41, 55–8, 135
interdependence 20, 34, 46, 69
interests 9, 166
international relations 12–15, 24, 75
intractable conflicts, *see under* conflict
intuition 94

Journal of Conflict Resolution 14–15, 70, 148

Kelman, Herb 13, 14, 161
Keynes, John Maynard 50–1
Kriesberg, Louis 32

language 86, 90–2, 96–8, 104–6, 126
League of Nations 12
learned helplessness 51
Leary, Timothy 174
legitimacy 129, 151
Leviathan 36
Lewicki, Roy 20
Lewin, Kurt 65–7, 69, 74, 83, 132, 162
Lippmann, Walter 100
Locke, John 149
Lorenz, Konrad 43–4, 45, 46, 47, 134–5

Man, the State, and War 42
Managerial Grid, The 11
Managing on the Edge 11
Marx, Karl 28, 35, 49–50, 51, 62
Maslow, Abraham 78
mass media 24
'med-arb' 21
mediation 14, 16, 19, 20, 21–2, 23, 24, 27–8, 105, 124, 148, 152, 153, 154, 155, 156–8, 159, 160, 161, 162, 165, 171
  Chinese 152
  defined 21
  oppression story 157–8
  satisfaction story 156–7
  social justice story 157
  transformation story 157
Mennonites 14
Milgram, Stanley 53–4, 95
Mill, James 150
Mill, John Stuart 150, 151, 153
Miller, Neal 51
Morgenstern, Oscar 70
Mouton, Jane 11, 108

nationalism 112–14, 115, 122, 139
needs 9, 13, 43, 46, 56–7, 62, 66, 76, 77–81, 84, 91, 100, 102–3, 104, 105, 114, 117–19, 120, 136, 151, 156, 166

negotiation 19, 20, 27, 86, 93, 103, 105, 114, 155, 156, 159, 160, 164, 166, 173
  defined 20
  principled 26
Negotiation Journal 20
neutrality 153–5, 158
Nicholson, Michael 82

objectivist school in conflict 34–5, 36
On Aggression 43
opportunity 4, 5, 6, 88, 168, 172–3, 174

paradigm shift 65, 75–7, 81–3, 148
Pascale, Robert Turner 11
peace movement 12–15
peacemaking 47–8
Peacemaking among Primates 46
perception 34, 67–9, 81–2, 86, 91–4, 106, 114–15
persuasion 26–7, 104
popular texts in conflict resolution 24–7
power 12, 13, 14, 40, 42, 75–6, 77–8, 79–80, 86, 104–6, 108–10, 120–1, 122, 124, 139, 165–8, 171–2, 173, 176
praxis 6
Prisoner's Dilemma 70–2
problem-solving workshops 13–14, 148, 153, 154, 155–6, 161–5, 167
procedural fairness, *see* process control
process control 23, 152, 157
Promise of Mediation, The 156
propaganda 87, 99–104, 110–14, 117, 118, 128, 139, 141, 142, 143
Pruitt, Dean 20, 80, 110, 120–2
public
  defined 100
  public opinion 99–104

Quakers 14

Rapaport, Anatol 14, 38–9, 70, 71
rational choice theory 82–3
representativeness 92–3
Rousseau, Jean Jacques 48–9, 50
Rubin, Jeffrey 110, 120–2

San Francisco Community Boards 16
Sandole, Dennis 75

Sapir–Whorf hypothesis 91
Schelling, Thomas 36
scientific management 10
Seligman, Martin 51
Simmel, Georg 33, 62–3, 65, 69, 70, 72, 83, 126, 148, 175
Simon, Herbert 4, 107
Sites, Paul 78–9
situational theories of conflict 32, 33–4
Skinner, Burrhus Frederic 52–3
Smith, Anthony 112
social comparison theory 98–9
social learning 54–5, 98
structural violence 32, 34
subjectivist school in conflict 35–6, 68
symbols 89–90

Taylor, Frederick W. 10
Territorial Imperative, The 45
territory 45–6
theories in use 61
Theory of Games and Economic Behavior 70
Thibaut, John 23
Thomas, W.I. 129
time perspective 36
trained incapacity 64
Tuchman, Barbara 117

ultimate attribution error 127
United Nations 8, 12, 24, 167
Ury, William 24, 25

Veblen, Thorstein 64
Vietnam War 6
Volkan, Vamik 131–2, 139, 161, 163–5, 166, 168

Walker, Laurens 23
Waltz, Kenneth 42
Webb, Keith 48
Weeks, Dudley 26
Wilson, Harold 13
win–win 25–6, 27, 72, 151, 161
workplace conflict 27, 28, 30, 32, 64, 101
Wright, Quincy 14

xenophobia 142–3